C000253192

NETTING FISHES

Fr JOHN TWIST SJ

NETTING FISHES
and other homilies

ST PAULS

Biblical quotations taken from *The Jerusalem Bible* © 1966 by Darton Longman & Todd Ltd and Doubleday and Company Ltd.

Line drawing by Vanessa Platt

Cover design by C.P. Ranger

ST PAULS Publishing
187 Battersea Bridge Road, London SW11 3AS, UK
www.stpaulspublishing.com

Copyright © ST PAULS 2009
ISBN 978-0-85439-757-0

A catalogue record is available for this book from the British Library.

Set by Tukan DTP, Stubbington, Fareham, UK
Printed and bound in Great Britain by Athenaeum Press Ltd,
Gateshead, Tyne & Wear, UK

ST PAULS is an activity of the priests and brothers
of the Society of St Paul who proclaim the Gospel
through the media of social communication

CONTENTS

Foreword

Later in life some adults moan about the times they were forced as children to sit through dreary religious services. They may even use this as a pretext for the abandonment of belief and faith. Some, no doubt, have genuinely been victims of irreverent or half hearted worship, defective liturgy, or banal and ill-prepared sermons, but, by and large, this is not an experience I have shared.

The parishes where I have lived have been blessed with gifted preachers. The schools I attended were places where faith was part of the fabric, and certainly never dull. And the priests who have been my friends are some of the finest men I know. From my childhood I still vividly recall some of the Jesuit priests who made sense for me of the endless complexities and challenges involved in growing up.

Netting Fishes – a collection of sermons delivered by Fr John Twist SJ, and some of which I heard when they were first delivered – comes from that same Ignatian tradition.

The best sermons are those that build on the rabbinical teaching tradition – where the story is used to illustrate a deeper truth. Such sermons successfully engage the heart and the head, emotions as well as intellect. Not everyone has this gift but John Twist has it in great measure.

As a school chaplain at a renowned international Jesuit College, on a daily basis he is confronted by bright young minds, questioning minds. He knows that merely repeating doctrine or offering pious platitudes is not enough.

From their very varied backgrounds, many of these young people, for whom these sermons were first written, have first hand experience of pain, confusion, disappointment, grief, brokenness, and the toxic loneliness that is such a hallmark of contemporary society. There is some comfort for them in the old belief that earth has no sorrow that heaven cannot heal. Happily, there is also idealism, energy, vitality, camaraderie, loyalty and hopefulness to counter the depredations of the Black Dog.

Fr John's Stonyhurst students are a demanding lot. What else would you expect from a school that has produced more Victoria Crosses and more saints than any other? This, too, was where Gerard Manley Hopkins crafted some of his poems, where J.R.R. Tolkien wrote some of *The Lord of the Rings*, whilst regularly visiting his son who taught at Stonyhurst.

Stonyhurst is a school where each year, on the feast day of St Edmund Campion, the rope with which this Elizabethan martyr was dragged to his execution at Tyburn is reverently carried by the Heads of Line to the altar where Mass will be celebrated. Knowing their history, knowing their story, helps today's young Christians understand that their religious liberties did not come without a price.

The sermons in this collection also give Catholics seeking to make sense of the confusing terrain of contemporary culture some helpful maps and a compass.

Fr John is a great walker: so charting a journey, knowing where you are going, comes naturally.

He hikes for miles over the Lancashire fells. He leads pilgrims to abandoned abbeys and to the remote fastnesses where ancient English saints discovered God and discovered what He wanted them to do with their lives.

Perhaps it was during some of those walks that some of the ideas used in these talks suggested themselves. What is certain is that every word is weighed and each sentence carefully considered. Prepared with great love and diligence, readers of all ages and backgrounds will gain something from them.

These sermons also sit well with the charism of Fr Pedro Arrupe, the twenty-eighth Superior General of the Society of Jesus, who famously said it was the task of Jesuits involved in education to form men and women for others. That is a thought that lies at the heart of this book.

Although the most important knowledge is knowledge of our own inadequacies, Cardinal John Henry Newman was right to remind us that if we waited until we were perfect, we would do nothing. *Netting Fishes* is not an invitation to wait until we are perfect, to be passive bystanders. It is a challenge to each of us to up our game.

An apocryphal story at Stonyhurst College has it that that the young Arthur Conan Doyle was punished after opening an umbrella during a sermon when more than words were pouring forth from the mouth of the preacher. Although a number of these sermons were also delivered in Stonyhurst's St Peter's church that is not a risk you will encounter in listening to Fr Twist. After reading *Netting Fishes* you will simply want more.

David Alton

Noticing God

The young boy Samuel does not recognise at first that God is calling him.

"Here I am, since you called me"

1 Samuel 3:6

In March 1943 the German submarines appeared to be winning the Battle of the Atlantic; in that month alone 140,000 tons of allied shipping were sunk by the dreaded U-boats. Then a sudden change struck: submarines found themselves ferreted out and attacked by allied aircraft even at dead of night. The German commanders had devices for detecting the allied radar, but all of a sudden they seemed useless. What had happened was that the allies had developed a radar with a wave-length of only 10cm, so small that the Germans not only did not know about it, but believed it impossible that such a radar could exist: hence they made no attempt to detect it. So great was the effect of the new radar in aircraft that in May 1943 two convoys crossed the ocean without the loss of a single ship whilst no less than forty submarines were sunk: from then on the Battle of the Atlantic was substantially won.

Young Samuel's problem was that he could not recognise the voice of God so that repeatedly he thought the voice must have some other explanation: like the German submarine crews his mind simply could not make sense of what was happening. And we are very much in the same position.

If one was to ask "When did you last hear God?" most of us would be puzzled: we rather think we've never "heard" God, and indeed we are a bit wary of anyone who thinks they have. Yet surely God who

11

upholds creation at every moment, who knows our every need, who is described by Jesus as "Our Father", must be trying to make some contact with us. Can it be that because we are not on his wavelength, we do not hear God? And if this is so, how do we detect the voice of God?

We are in contact with God more by our senses than through our brains; in certain moods we become aware of God's presence, albeit in a hazy way. What is more, to some extent we can attune ourselves to be in touch with God. This is a delicate matter and it only comes with practice: most religious things that we do – going to Mass, saying prayers, reading one of the psalms, even noticing a lovely day – can put us in contact with God; very often however we do not realise this is happening to us. Here are some dos and don'ts for becoming aware of God:

– Do try to cultivate the right atmosphere. There is a lot gained for example by going to church early, taking time to settle down, saying a few familiar prayers.

– Do take your own feelings seriously. All too easily, we suppose that God has more important things to do than bother with us, so that the feelings we have when we pray are ignored.

– Don't assume that God always touches us through pleasant feelings: sometimes that nagging voice telling us we are not being true to ourselves is from above.

– Don't look for special effects. Far from speaking to us through thunder and lightning, God tends to be the tiny voice within that we barely advert to.

- Do try to notice the pious experiences you have had, and use these as a rough guide for detecting the divine voice. For example many of us find Christmas a very religious experience: well what is it we feel then? Note this and expect similar feelings.

- Do practice religion. Samuel found God eventually because first, he was in the right place, the temple; second, he tried again and again to work out what was happening; third, he had a religious guide, Eli.

- Finally do not suppose that you will get a message from God. You may do, but more common is a gentle awareness of his presence, comforting, reassuring and natural.

Homily given on 2nd Sunday of Ordinary Time in year "B" at St. Aloysius' Glasgow.

Christian Unity

Christian Unity should be seen as a
necessity, not an option.

"Now you together are Christ's body"
1 Corinthians 12:27

Christmas is beginning to fade from our minds now,
yet it is interesting how we can often retain memories
of the way it was many years ago. Perhaps some of us
can remember those primitive Christmas tree lights
that we used to string up each year, made up of just
one wire with sockets attached for the tiny bulbs. If
only one bulb was missing or broken, none of the
others would work; and this was because the single
wire carried the electric current through each bulb
on to the next. Thus all the bulbs were vital, each
must work in order to make the circuit complete.

Paul is telling us that it is like that with Jesus
Christ. Christ is like the electric current bringing
light and life to the world. But our Lord does not
operate like a flash of lightning, streaking down to
one place or another. Our Lord's power travels
through his body, through us his followers: if we are
broken up, divided, separated from one another, then
his grace cannot move and is made ineffective.

So let us be clear in this week of prayer for
Christian Unity: our unity is vital; we cannot
function otherwise. Christian Unity is not some
hobby for those who are interested in that sort of
thing. We must be together or we cannot be the
functioning body of Christ.

What fundamentally unites us is our common
baptism, which makes all Christians members of the
one body of Christ. And we can give thanks to God

that the relations between Churches are so much more friendly nowadays, as we are able to acknowledge the presence of our Lord in other Christians. Nevertheless, Christians live in a sort of impaired union: our legs may not be broken, but we are limping. What can we do to help bring true and full unity to the body of Christ?

First, we should avoid all disparaging talk about other churches and denominations. There may well be disagreements between us, but we can still respect the sincerity and honesty of Christians from whom we differ.

Second, we will find it helpful to actually visit other Churches. It is one of the most concrete ways to discover how much we really do have in common.

Third, perhaps most important, we must avoid divisions and quarrelling among ourselves, being careful to accept the leadership of our Bishops, and seeking to work with each other in harmony and love.

Homily given on 3rd Sunday of Ordinary Time in year "C" at St. Aloysius' Glasgow.

All for Free

We can lose the world through trying to grab it; it is already free and only needs to be accepted gratefully.

"Theirs is the Kingdom of Heaven"
Matthew 5:3

It may be thought that Western civilisation, even after 2,000 years of Christianity, is driven by grab and by greed. The Indian Fakir, Gandhi, on being asked what he thought of Christianity, quipped that he thought it would be a good idea! To him, as to many greatly moved by the Buddha's light, the great flaw in human nature is desire: craving things. Craving them so much that we destroy ourselves to get them; wanting them so much that we do not notice we have them anyway!

Gandhi's favourite Hindu saying runs:

> *All this world must be pervaded by a Lord,*
> *Renounce it and enjoy it.*

As Gandhi pointed out, Western civilisation, with its marketing, advertising, promoting, creates fake needs, what he called "manufactured want", and then leaves us dissatisfied because we never seem to have enough. Were he asked about the National Lottery, Gandhi might have pointed out how a compulsive craving to be rich devours a person's soul.

Great speculation developed in the nineteenth century about the schooling of Jesus, and extraordinary views were advanced. One of these was that Jesus spent the thirty or so years of his early life as a

16

Buddhist monk in Tibet! Pretty dubious by any standards, but it brings out something a lot of people have noticed regarding Jesus. He seems to be so other-worldly; so detached from ambition, greed, self-seeking: as is shown more than anywhere in his Sermon on the Mount.

The teaching of Jesus is that God is with us bestowing his gifts: a humble acceptance of this leads a person to recognise how blest we are. Like Adam and Eve in the Garden of Eden we can enjoy everything free, until we begin to grab and snatch; then all is ruined.

How fortunate are those who recognise the closeness of God, be they rich or poor, mighty or powerless; who know that all this world must be pervaded by a Lord: they can renounce it and then enjoy it.

Homily given on 4th Sunday of Ordinary Time in year "A" at St. Aloysius' Glasgow.

Ordinary People

God detects natural qualities in us that many would despise. We need to believe that he can make use of us, even though we be but ordinary people.

"Do not be afraid, from now on it is people you will catch"
Luke 5:10

On 11 February 1858 Bernadette Soubirous, a diminutive fourteen-year-old sickly girl, saw near a stream what she first took to be a ghost; in subsequent days her descriptions suggested she was having visions of the Mother of God.

We need to bear in mind that that this happened in nineteenth-century France, which more than most places, was blossoming with "modern" ideas. With the growth of education, science, enlightened attitudes, better off people were at last casting off mediaeval superstitions, and adopting rational, scientific attitudes to life. The local Lourdes' officials were freethinkers, possibly tolerant of religion but certainly contemptuous of it.

To them, therefore, Bernadette represented the classic example of a dying breed: of rural peasant stock, virtually illiterate, malnourished and sickly, and, as it would appear, utterly credulous. The early disciples of Jesus seemed like that: simple fishermen, unversed in the ways of the world – ask them to speak in front of a crowd and they would stutter and stammer helplessly.

It would seem therefore that our Lord calls inadequate people, in order to show his power through them: since they are so weak the great works

18

they are to do will display his heavenly strength. How privileged they were to be given such dignity, whilst lacking special ability; these disciples were to change the world, although they would never have got elected to the local village council.

Nevertheless such people are not changed into Zombies, carrying out the heavenly diktat. Our Lord in a subtle and gentle way discovers strengths in persons, which he brings forth so that in the event they prove to have a natural aptitude for the very things which seem so beyond them.

Thus Bernadette may have been small and shy; very vulnerable before the intimidating officials who interrogated her about the mysterious Lady: how frightening when people suggested she must be out of her mind! But with a gut peasant stubbornness Bernadette stuck to her story, however often she was questioned, and regardless of the sneers or innuendoes of the great and the good. It was that very stubborn honesty that convinced in the end: her lack of education, the absence of smooth talk, gave her a down to earth reliability that many intellectual people do not have.

So too the first disciples doubtless lacked the oratory of a Paul, the learning of a Gamaliel, but they knew a thing or two about catching fish; and Jesus with a sympathetic kindness hints that this is just what he is looking for. In time they will find their natural powers coming to fruition in netting souls for the kingdom.

Therefore, if the Lord calls you don't simply decide you are inadequate, of course you are in a sense. Who is adequate to represent him as a Religious Sister or a Priest? But he can draw out from your personality hidden strengths, ones you never recognised: trust him and you will find your true self!

Homily given on 5th Sunday of Ordinary Time in year "C" at St. Aloysius' Glasgow.

The Cost of Caring

Jesus paid a price for the miracles he worked. He ended up swopping places with the rejected.

"He had to stay outside in places where nobody lived"
Mark 1:40

The leper had to stay away from towns and villages because of the danger of contaminating others with his disease; indeed the word "Leper" has become almost proverbial for someone who is an outcast.

Our society has many of these lepers, or outcasts: they may be asylum seekers, the insane, problem families that eventually get quarantined to sink housing estates. We are not that different from other times in this respect. Happily serious efforts are being made to integrate people better. Schools are encouraged to take all kinds of children, buildings are adapted to take wheelchairs and so on.

Jesus did not merely accept the outcast leper, he actually cured him, but at a price. For we are told that Jesus himself could "no longer enter any town, but had to stay where nobody lived"; and we are given constant hints that Jesus became a reject, as though he had swopped places with the leper he healed. Eventually he could only work in the countryside; the triumphal entry into Jerusalem was during daylight hours, at night he needed to go to friends in Bethany to avoid arrest. When he was crucified it was outside the city: a total reject.

And if we think about it, we can see why. The leper is feared because his disease could spread and undermine society. A person of true goodness, no more fits in than does a leper: he too is a threat to ways of life that have become used to evil, adapted to it, that has accepted bad ways as an inevitable part of life. To really do good is to subvert society.

Consider what this implies if you are to follow Jesus. Think how many saints were, at least in their lifetimes, rejected. Mother Teresa began by leaving her smart Loretto Convent, and working alone on the streets; John Ogilvie and the missionaries who came to seventeenth-century Scotland, had to live as hunted men; Dietrich Bonhoeffer of the German Confessing Church, ended up in a concentration camp and was eventually executed.

The serious follower of Jesus can not only accept those who are popularly cast out, they can even heal them; but they may well be rejected themselves.

Homily given on 6th Sunday of Ordinary Time of year "B" in St. Aloysius' Glasgow,

Unwelcome Message

We feel inadequate to spread Jesus'
message, but then so did his first disciples.

*"Fixing his eyes on his disciples,
Jesus spoke"*
Luke 6:20

There is a crowd of listless, weary people, waiting for
something. Then there is you, one of the chosen, one
who is to hear the heavenly message, and afterwards
pass it on to those helpless waiting people. It is to
you, that Jesus says "Happy are the poor, the hungry,
the sad, the harassed." This, would you believe it, is
the heavenly message that you must declare to the
waiting world.

My guess is that you do not feel comfortable to
spread this message; and you do not feel comfortable
because you hardly believe it. Like most people
around us, we strive to believe in the material dream:
that money, security, feeling good, being acceptable:
these are the way of happiness. Maybe there is a dull
feeling that our possessions based society does not
fully work, but we have learnt to live with it, and
hope for little else. In this situation we can hardly see
ourselves telling the crowd how fortunate they
would be to be poor, hungry, sad and harassed!

If it is any comfort, our position is exactly that
of the first disciples. They admired Jesus, but found
his message baffling, even embarrassing. They, or
most of them, stayed with him because they had an
inkling that there must be truth in it somehow.

And yet some people have seen the truth of
Jesus' message, have adopted it and found it works.
What is more such people do persuade the waiting

masses of the truth of Jesus. St Francis of Assisi, realised that his wealth was a sham, a delusion, a snare. Dramatically he gave away everything, even the clothes he was wearing, and abandoned his way of life. Francis was able to speak the message of Jesus, because he lived that message, and found that it worked. What is more people believed him: they realised that the way of Jesus does bring peace and happiness, whilst the claims of prosperity are an illusion.

Honesty requires us to admit, that we only pay lip service to the powerful declaration of Jesus; we barely believe that the poor, hungry, sad and harassed are to inherit the earth. But we must do our best to enter into this deep mysterious truth our Lord proclaims: that the world with its claims to wealth as the road to happiness is living an illusion; that we must rely on God; that real joy is a gift, not a possession; that in the divine plan God's kingdom will be given to those in need, to those who are humble, to the patient, to those who know they need God; and that wealth is no substitute for God.

If we can, even in a weak way, hold and believe the teaching of Jesus; then we will be able to do what he commands us: announce his truth to a desperately needy, waiting world.

Homily given on 7th Sunday of Ordinary Time in year "C" at St. Aloysius' Glasgow,

Surviving Disappointment

Even if we experience terrible tragedy,
there is still hope in our Christian Faith.

*"The time will come for the bridegroom
to be taken away"*
Mark 2:20

Priests may not get married, but they do see a great variety of weddings, usually very happy events, but not always. I was once involved in the preparation of a couple for their marriage: the date was fixed, details worked out, everything was getting lined up. Then one evening as they were crossing a street together – it was January, dark with snow on the roads – a driver, perhaps confused by the glare of the snow and ice, accidentally hit the woman, but somehow left the man untouched. Within seconds his fiancé was lying in the road, and as he soon found out to his horror, she was dead. The wedding that had been planned ended up as her funeral, which he attended.

The dreadful experience of that poor man brings home the strange warning of Jesus to his friends: rejoice and celebrate, but be ready for a day when a great loss may come. We believe that the disciples in general enjoyed being with Jesus, as so they should; but they were utterly shattered and defeated when he was arrested, tortured and killed. They panicked and ran away.

We cannot really prepare for such disasters, nor can we by our own power cope with them. Who knows what shattering experience some of us here may have at a point in life? Who can be so foolish as to lay out a remedy in advance for such tragedies? All we can do is hope that the Lord may lift us up again when we are defeated, as after his resurrection he rescued Peter, Mary Magdalene and the others from despair.

For the good news is this, that Jesus went through a most terrible experience, apparently defeated by evil, but won over it by rising from the dead. To believe in him is to know that there is always hope. Like that young couple who were planning to marry, we cannot guarantee that disaster will never strike: what we can say with certainty is that any calamity can be conquered by Christ who shares his resurrection power with us.

Homily given on 8th Sunday of Ordinary Time in year "B" at St. Aloysius' Glasgow.

Healthy Visions

Pendle Hill, near Clitheroe in Lancashire, is famous for witches. Yet it has a more serious religious claim as the place where George Fox had a kind of vision in 1652.

"God chose to reveal his son in me"
Galatians 1:16

Paul is very keen to insist to the Galatians that he is not dependent on the other Apostles for his knowledge of Jesus Christ; he got it, he claims, by a direct divine revelation.

This desire to claim direct revelations from on high is a strong one, because then it can be asserted that then one's beliefs must be right. Moses, on the Mountain, Muhammad in his cave, Paul going to Damascus, all have life-changing experiences which they are convinced are real encounters with God.

Listen, for example to this startling story:

As we travelled we came near a very great hill, called Pendle Hill, and I was moved of the Lord to go up to the top of it; which I did with difficulty, it was so very steep and high. When I was come to the top, I saw the sea bordering upon Lancashire. From the top of this hill the Lord let me see in what places he had a great people to be gathered. At night we came to an inn, and declared truth to the man of the house, and wrote a paper to the priests and professors, declaring the day of the Lord, and that Christ was come to teach people Himself, by His power and Spirit in their hearts, and to bring people off from all the world's ways and teachers, to His own free teaching, who had bought them, and was the Saviour of all them that believed in Him. The man of the house spread the paper abroad, and was mightily affected with the truth. Here the Lord opened unto me, and let me see a great people in white raiment by a river side, coming to the Lord; and the place that I saw them in was about Wensleydale and Sedbergh.

That is from George Fox the founder of the Quakers, and refers to a kind of vision he had in 1652.

Although the general mood of modern people is to be suspicious of these revelations, and perhaps wisely so, we need to be aware that there are increasing numbers of groups that do claim such visions; and often of a very eccentric kind, claiming to know when the world will end, of cosmic battles about to take place, Armageddon and all that. How in this morass can we sort out the true visionary from the fanatic? How keep faith, and yet avoid craziness?

I suggest the answer is this: Paul accepted that if his revelation was valid it would have to harmonise with the teaching of the other Apostles; he was not into founding some religious sect of his own! We can have a sound and sensible faith, if we ensure that it keeps in with the belief of the Universal Church, spread through the ages and believed all over the world.

Homily given on 9th Sunday of Ordinary Time in year "C" at Stonyhurst College, Lancs.

Clothes

Accepting who we really are is humbling,
but puts us in touch with reality.

"Who told you that you were naked?"
Genesis 3:11

No reference to the present company, but one of the ugliest of sights is the human body! We wear clothes not merely for warmth and beautification, but to disguise the very embarrassing fact that we look remarkably like chimpanzees.

Truth to tell we are our clothes, and not much else. When the dying Cardinal Wolsey said "If I had but served my God as I have served my king, he would not have left me naked to mine enemies", he was using a way of speech which betrays the fact that nakedness is a symbol of helplessness, weakness, vulnerability. If you want to find out what a person is, do not look at their body, look at their clothes. Victorian men had a very strong sense of their own importance – hence the top hat; the Nazis were instinctive bullies – hence the jackboot; kings and queens purport to rule over people – hence their crowns.

That saying we have: "If such and such be true I'll eat my hat" means the real me is the hat I wear, and since if I'm wrong I will have to swallow my pride, it is my hat that must be chewed up.

So the discovery by Adam and Eve that they were naked was a painful realisation that they had nothing, were terribly vulnerable, weak and helpless: the voice of God sounded like the roar of a lion and they hid in fear.

They had, of course, been naked all the time, but

until now they were blissfully unaware of it; like a child absorbed in its own world.

There are three ways we can live with our nakedness. The first is in innocence where like Adam and Eve we simply have no concern for ourselves. A wonderful state: very few enjoy it.

The second is the state of pride where a person pretends to be important, strong, special, independent, self-reliant. Pride works very well so long as no one pricks the bubble: the famous Emperor who had no clothes remained blissfully ignorant of his state because the courtiers were afraid to tell him; unfortunately a child blurted out the question "Mummy why hasn't that man any clothes?" and the Emperor was, literally, exposed.

The third is the state of humility. It means accepting our weaknesses, but accepting too that God cares for and sustains us. Jesus died naked on the cross, weak and helpless, just like in the manger; but he relied on his heavenly Father, and thus showed that strange strength, courage and confidence that goes with humility.

Homily given on 10th Sunday of Ordinary Time in year "B" at Stonyhurst College, Lancs.

Consequences

We necessarily build up our personalities as good or bad, and this character persists in us after death.

"For the things we did in the body"
2 Corinthians 5:10

In the west few people believe in re-incarnation, and those who do are often considered slightly nutty. But serious Christian commentators have admitted the notion that persons are repeatedly re-born in one form or another is by no means stupid. For if we are to believe in a future life at all, it is pretty naive to suppose that we will not be the same kind of person in the next life as we are in this; and that means we must take all our emotional baggage with us – our hates, our greed, our attitudes, our affections.

All of us would readily admit that our day to day physical activities store up consequences for tomorrow: drink too much – you have a hangover; eat the wrong food and too much of it – you become overweight, strain the heart etc. Even the famous James Bond is told by M. at one point that the good life is ruining his effectiveness as a "double 0" agent, and he is sent to a health farm, to get rid of his free radicals. So why suppose that our moral activity: the right things we do, the wrongs we commit, simply evaporate. They don't; they build up in our personalities, just like fat, or free radicals, nicotine and so on.

Those people who do not care for their bodies, but overeat, over drink and avoid exercise, do so because they are only thinking of the here and now. Indulgence is pleasant at the time, leave aside the later consequences, it will seem very fulfilling. If a person looks to the future, then they are very careful how they act in the present, for it is in the now that we lay the foundations for the days to come.

This is what is so forceful in St Paul's letter. "To be in the body, is to be exiled from the Lord", he says. His whole longing is for that future time when he will be with Christ, and so he has little interest in bogging down in present pleasantries. This is the attitude we must attain, for the day will come when we will quite literally meet Our Lord: it could be the most pleasant of encounters, or it could be a dreadful, devastating shock. Perhaps the reason we are not re-incarnated is that the meeting with Christ so penetrates our personality that we either are purified of all bad attitudes in an instant; or become overwhelmed and repulsed by his sheer goodness that we avert from him utterly.

But at least we must genuinely strive like Paul to think of the Future. The day will come when I will meet, face to face, the man who died for me; the man who is both my creator and my brother. Will I be ready? Am I taking steps to become ready?

Homily given on 11th Sunday of Ordinary Time in year "B" at Stonyhurst College, Lancs.

Be There!

It is in being close to Jesus that we will be influenced by him.

"Master, we are going down!"
Mark 4:39

The proverbial Jolly Jack Tar stationed on a gun deck of a ship of the line in October 1805 waiting for battle to be joined, sure in the knowledge that the result would be huge flying splinters, decapitated limbs, operations conducted without anaesthetic in the bowels of the ship: that proverbial Jolly Jack Tar would perhaps not have been greatly amused to know that the advice Admiral Horatio Nelson had given his captains before the battle was "that anyone who lays his ship close against the enemy will be doing the right thing".

But Nelson knew his business. Those wooden sailing ships with their cast iron cannon were not much more than drifting logs, and the only way to win any battle was to get them in the thick of things and hope for the best. Small wonder such horrific injuries resulted.

We Christians very much prefer to follow Christ at a distance; we are touchline supporters, rather than full blooded players. And our attitude is very understandable, for those who were close to him quickly found that the going was apt to get rough. Get into an open boat with Jesus and look what happens.

And yet cheering from a safe distance, means that whilst we do not get into danger with Christ, we do not experience his power either. In the apocryphal Gospel of St Thomas Jesus says, "He who is close to me is close to the fire". The apostles were only able to say in admiration "Who can this be, even the wind and the sea obey him?" after they had been terrified out of their wits.

There is a practical lesson in this we might well remember. It may be that at some point in life we go through a terrible experience: a death, divorce, an incurable illness diagnosed. It will seem at that time that we are in the thick of trouble, whilst our Lord is simply not there. "Lord, do you not care?" will be the agitated thought in our hearts. But it is at those times that He is most present, quietly in control of everything; for even the wind and the sea obey him.

Homily given on 12th Sunday of Ordinary Time in year "B" at Saints Peter & Paul, Mitcham.

Clashing Kingdoms

Jesus is setting up a Kingdom that is mysterious, but powerful. It is not to be ignored, because another such Kingdom is already in place. The two will necessarily clash.

"The Spirit came down on him like a dove"
Mark 1:10

The first person chosen to be king in Israel was Saul, and when he was anointed king, the Spirit came down on him and he went into an ecstasy. He became a changed man, and from being an obscure farmer, morphed into a powerful leader who defeated Israel's enemies in battle.

In Israel a person was a king not by inheritance, but through divine choice. A king was anointed by a prophet, and received heavenly power to act in God's name and with God's own strength. Hence He was known as "The Lord's Anointed", or "The Christ". So understand that when the Spirit came down on Jesus of Nazareth at his baptism in the Jordan, he was being anointed King, he was made The Christ.

This is certainly how Jesus understood the event, for this carpenter's son then took to going around acting, as it would seem to other people, with considerable arrogance, as though he was a king. Further he claimed to be founding a kingdom, that he called the Kingdom of God. When he was executed the notice on the cross would say sarcastically "Jesus of Nazareth, the King of the Jews".

But this kingdom, which Jesus claimed to rule, was an odd one. It did not seem to have an army; there was no territory, no area with borders over which to rule. The king had no palace, but appeared to follow a wandering lifestyle: no base, no capital city. Even the laws of this kingdom were only passed from mouth to mouth. In so far as it meant anything it was about personal influence: for there was no doubt this self styled King Jesus could draw the crowds, sway multitudes, even expel disease. And he said his followers would do the same.

So is this something new, never seen before? No it is not. There is already an invisible kingdom around, unacknowledged but wielding immense power: it is the kingdom of Satan. There is no army, no territory, no palace; but it is there. It wields influence; it controls; it is destructive of human life. If this newly anointed man from Nazareth thinks he can set up his God Kingdom, he will get a shock: something opposite to it is already in place. As we proceed with Saint Mark's Gospel this term, we will see a showdown coming: there will not be room for both kingdoms.

You may think you can just watch from the sidelines, as Jesus strives to plant the Kingdom of God in people. But you cannot. You have to join one side or the other side. At this very moment a battle is taking place within you; you may be totally unaware of it; it is the battle to establish God's kingdom or Satan's kingdom in your personality. No one is outside. The good news, and we will hear this in the weeks ahead, is that Jesus, now anointed as the Messiah, the Christ, has power to overwhelm the Satan.

Homily given on the Feast of the Baptism of our Lord in Year "B" at Stonyhurst College, Lancs.

Power in Poverty

There is a strange wealth in having nothing;
it is to be free to enjoy everything.

"Carry no purse, no haversack"
Luke 10:4

An ancient Hindu religious writing declares:

> "All this world must be pervaded by a Lord;
> renounce it, and enjoy it"

An early Christian writer says things that may clarify
the mystery Hindu saying. Of Christians he says:

> "Though they are residents at home in their
> own countries, their behaviour is that of
> transients. For them any foreign country is a
> motherland, and any motherland is a foreign
> country. Their days are passed on the earth,
> but their citizenship is above in the heavens."

If one is not addicted to the visible things; if one can
be free of them, then we find there is a hidden power
pervading the world – "all this world must be
pervaded by a Lord". And this is what Jesus was
showing his friends as he sent them off on their first
mission: "carry no purse, no haversack, go empty
handed; but through your very poverty you will pass
God's riches to the sick and disturbed".

Since the time of our Lord, numbers of
Christians have tried to follow his way by forming
groups who bound themselves by religious vows:
poverty to be free of possessiveness, celibacy to be
free to serve everyone, obedience to be liberated
from one's own ego. Perhaps we underestimate the

importance of these groups: did you know that there are over one million religious committed in this way in the world today? Ranging from Mother Teresa's Sisters among the destitute on the streets of Calcutta, to Carthusian Monks living as virtual hermits in isolated places.

And surely our world desperately needs people who have this insight: people who can see that to win the National Lottery is not half as lucky as to lose it; people who don't despise the rich, but do despise riches, and therefore do not despise the poor; people who can see that lust is a form of selfishness, but sacrifice a form of love; people who want a higher ideal than the voice of their own egos.

The disciples came back rejoicing: "even the devils submit to us when we use your name", and Jesus told them "I saw Satan fall like lightning from heaven". Though they had no credit card, no American Express, no Armani suits, no Gucci shoes, somehow an awful lot had come about through them.

Homily given on 14th Sunday of Ordinary Time in year "C" at St. Aloysius' Glasgow,

Grow!

We should ask: 'What kind of soil is my faith growing in?" Then consider how we should act.

"Others fell on rich soil and produced their crop"
Matthew 13:8

Life is pointless. Each of us is like an empty field: just there, waiting for something to happen. To fill the vacuum we invent things to do: we seek some kind of fulfilment, pursue a career, have our favourite sport, make friends with others, go on holiday. Just as a garden left to itself will automatically sprout all sorts of things, weeds and flowers, brambles and bushes, so do we invent a great variety of things, maybe good, maybe harmful to fill out our lives.

Unknown to us perhaps, our field can be given its real purpose: it is there so that the Word of God can be sown in it. If that Word takes root and flourishes we will fulfil the reason for our creation. And because the Word of God is sown in our field where we are already sprouting all sorts of other plants, there may well be a competition going on between God's life and all those other things growing alongside it.

For as our Lord explains, our life choices make our field the kind of place in which God's Word must seek to take root: possibly stony, possibly shallow, possibly thorny, possibly fertile. Let us look at two types of Catholic in whom the Word must try to grow:

– The cultural Catholic has a strong sense of belonging: perhaps of immigrant background, with some very devout relatives, a tendency to mix allsorts of things together: the school they went to, a certain football team, the church and priests they know, and regard it as Christianity. In such a person the seed does grow, but the soil is shallow! Move that man or woman to an environment that is non-supportive of religion, away from their family and roots, and their religion vanishes. It has no depth.

– The worldly Catholic is rather the opposite. Perhaps grew up in a very traditional home, then got a good education, went to college, now has a successful career. Intelligent, articulate, at ease with modern life. Their very success leads them into a world where religion, and especially its demands in personal morality, is seen as a hindrance: alright for simple folk, but not adjusted to the world of success, liberation and prosperity. For such a person the Word of God may be strangled: the faith once held gets choked by the aggressive growth of other ideas that come to take over.

Now the question is, should our field be in one of these two conditions, what can we DO about it?

1. If you have a shallow faith, you must try to deepen it. Do not just drift along with a set of comfortable practices learnt in childhood. If the best you can do is claim that you have held onto the religion you grew up with, then you are not growing. Plants that do not grow will die.

2. Your problem is more serious if you find you are leaving your religion behind, as you move into the

happy world of material success. There is a lot of good in all sorts of things, but the only ultimate good, the only thing that will really last, is God's Word. You must choose! Either the thorns will strangle your religion, or you must cast off the thorns: it is up to you.

The reward for those who do truly and deeply accept the Word of God is growth: the real proof of life: thirty-fold, sixty-fold, one hundred-fold.

Homily given on 15th Sunday of Ordinary Time in year "A" at St. Aloysius' Glasgow.

Moral Defects

Physical perfection, does not make a person good. We make our good or bad choices in spite of our physical condition. It is these choices which really affect us and our society.

"An enemy has done this"
Matthew 13:28

Walking through a field of wheat today, it is striking that there are simply no weeds: modern technology with its special chemical sprays can ensure that only the good stuff is permitted to sprout. Indeed with genetic advances special super strains of wheat can be grown resistant to disease, pest and blight.

There is a growing contrast, is there not, between the world of Jesus where good and evil are accepted because there is not much you can do about it, and modern science in which we can increasingly identify weaknesses and eliminate them? Why put up with good and bad, healthy and diseased, strong and weak, when you can choose the good, the strong, the healthy? The consequence, as we know, is that we are moving into a brave new world, where, for those who have no moral objection, the darnel can be rooted out before birth.

Let us pretend that a hundred years ago all these fantastic developments in genetics had already taken place. A couple in a small Austrian town are told that the embryo the wife is carrying has excellent prospects: he (for it is a boy) will have remarkable piercing blue eyes, will be of above average physique, possess a strong personality, be very courageous, and of good intelligence. In these circumstances they choose to have the child.

Sure enough the baby turns out exactly as described. They Christen him Adolf and are fascinated to see that every detail predicted for him comes true: but slowly a terrifying truth starts to come home to them. Their darling son, like every other human, can make his own choices. He turns out perfect alright, a perfect monster. Adolf Hitler, the man who grew up to murder millions and plunge the whole world into war, chose to pervert his endowment.

This is what Jesus knew, and what the modern world forgets: if we were simply animals, perfection would just be a matter of breeding; be we are not! Human beings are like gods: each man, each woman has a mind of their own. We are spiritual creatures, we make choices; they have tremendous consequences. The awful burden and privilege each of us carries is that we are the makers of our own destiny.

There is no magic way of getting rid of evil. All we can say is that in God's shrewd plan everything will eventually work for good. In this life we must be patient and trust in him.

Homily given on 16th week of Ordinary Time in year "A" at St. Aloysius' Glasgow.

Share!

All too often society is built on violence. We need a new kind of society based on trust and sharing.

"Where can we get bread for these people?"
John 6:5

The nasty war in Liberia brings home to us how disastrous human community can be. People very often just cannot get on together, and at its worst life degenerates into war, murder, rape and destruction. History shows that Liberia is by no means unique: I wonder how many people who are told there are over seven hundred castles in Wales, ever ask themselves why? They were hardly built to provide a tourist attraction six hundred years afterwards! Surely they bear witness to the extreme violence of their times, when everyone was in danger unless heavily protected. In reality our society sits on a volcano of violence, ready to explode at any moment, and unstoppable when it does.

In contrast, today's Gospel tells us of a highly significant action of Jesus: he forms a new community in the desert living from Divine providence. This people will have enough because God will provide for them, and each will have sufficient because they will share what they have. This society will be the alternative to that lifestyle of war and violence that bedevils mankind. The people realise how wonderful it all is, and even though their reaction in wanting to make Jesus King is overenthusiastic, they have correctly grasped that something truly epoch making has occurred.

44

No doubt if I were to suggest that the present mayhem in Liberia is your fault and my fault, you would feel indignant; but there is a degree to which it is true. We have failed to build that kingdom of peace which Jesus began, and as a result the clash of war tears up helpless people. We have obligations to help build the new society Jesus founded. What must we do?

We must work for a society that trusts in God. It is not a case of saying that all science, economics, hard work are mistaken; it is a matter of realising that the measly five barley loaves and two fish that we can make ourselves will only go round when a higher power blesses our efforts. When we see that God provides we are grateful; when we imagine it is every man for himself, we create the rat race.

We must share. Those five thousand simply had enough. No one ended up a fat cat from the meal; no one starved. Our divided society makes for a rival society, generating differing factions that come to fight each other. Can we Christians really claim that we are working for a fair society, rather than merely fighting our corner?

Ask yourself: what am I doing with my five loaves and two fish? Think of specific ways you can help build a sharing community, and put them into practice.

Homily given on 17th Sunday of Ordinary Time of year "B" at St. Aloysius' Glasgow.

Real Life

There is a higher kind of life than the one we have got used to.

"That which comes down from heaven and gives life to the world"
John 6:33

I soon began to feel there was something strange about the visitor. Perhaps it was the bright green skin, or the way he laughed uncontrollably when I peeled potatoes, maybe it was his strange habit of addressing me as "Earthling!"

"Yes," he said, "You earthlings think you can visit our planet with your space rockets and things, but the fact is we have been watching you lot for some time; indeed we have been trying to communicate with you." I pointed out that we British were not into space exploration by rocket, our speciality being hot air balloons, but he was not impressed.

"The trouble with you earthlings," he continued, "is that you just live a few years and then die. It is not meant to be like that you know; where I come from we live for ever. What's more you earthlings don't realise that you are not meant to have this puny little existence; you are made for greater things."

"That may well be so," I countered, "but in recent years our scientists have made great advances towards eternal life: new pills, replacement limbs, lots of care improvements. We reckon that soon most people will go on to over a hundred."

At this the little green man exploded in anger. "I'm not talking about lingering, I'm talking about

46

life: real life, eternal life, the life you were made for; the life to be given you from above."

"How do I get hold of that? Well, you have to believe; because the precious gift is full of twists and turns that will puzzle you earthlings. Unless you get heaven belief you will become discouraged and give up. You see heaven life is almost the opposite to what you call life, and for that reason it is caught in ways that seem strange. For example, dying is one of the ways to it; suffering is part of the path to it; but most of all heaven belief is not this earthling belief piffle."

It was a pity that the stranger had to go. I was about to explain to him that things are not that bad down here. But then perhaps it is just as well I did not attempt to; for I noticed that the only thing he took away from our wonderful planet as his saucer lifted off was, attached to it, a parking ticket.

Homily given on 18th Sunday of Ordinary Time in year "B" at St. Aloysius' Glasgow.

The Rear View

We only see part of the picture, and that is the part passing us by as we look backwards on life; another person is at the front, and we must allow him to steer.

"He who has come from God has seen the Father, and he alone"
John 6:46

Nowadays we are all experts on dinosaurs, but our Victorian forebears were puzzled and mystified by them. They could see that the creatures were huge, whilst their brains seemed small. For one real monster, the theory was proposed that since its tail was so far from its head, the brute must have had two brains: one in its head and the other in its tail. A good job there was no divorce in those days!

In fact we have a slight imitation of the principle in certain very heavy duty low loaders which have steering both at the front and at the back: the two drivers must co-ordinate their skills very closely, but given that, the special vehicle can negotiate its way round major twists and bends.

What our Lord is telling us is that he can see and understand things which are blind to us. We are like a person at the back of a long low loader gazing backwards, as life unfurls past us: We know what has happened, he at the front knows what is going to happen. It does not mean that we are stupid, or have no minds of our own; but it does mean that our knowledge is, so to speak, in arrears.

Perhaps the great challenge in life is to both think for oneself and also to believe; it is a matter of realising that we do have minds of our own, and ought to put them to good use; but at the same time realising there is much we do not know, and must be prepared to be guided. Religion is that wonderful knack of steering the back of the vehicle in such a way that it co-ordinates with the steerer at the front; that driver being Christ.

A quick glance at human history will show us the sad consequences of forgetting that we only control the rear of the vehicle of human history: we make a great mess of the world, we make a great mess of our personal lives, if we do not bear in mind that there is another driver; and he is in the front.

Homily given on 19th Sunday of Ordinary Time in year "B" at St. Aloysius' Glasgow.

Discouragement

We should expect some confusion in the
Christian life; but we must still keep faith.

***"Keep running steadily in the race we
have started"***
Hebrews 12:1

The Christians who are addressed in the letter to the
Hebrews, appear to be a group of converts who are
becoming discouraged. Their initial enthusiasm as
they adopted Christianity, had faded in the course of
time, and some of them were beginning to wish they
had remained in the Jewish Synagogue.

When we ourselves now look back on that
period after Vatican II, most of us can remember a
mood of excitement, even euphoria. The Mass would
be in English: at last people would be able to
understand it; no doubt new converts would come
flooding in now that everything was comprehensible.
The Scriptures now opened up to Catholics, a move
that would make us much more acceptable to other
Christian Churches. A readiness to accept modern
science and thought: surely this would result in a
general acceptance of the Catholic view as sensible
and acceptable. Such was the mood and expectation
of so many at that time.

And now forty years later quite a lot of
disillusion. The antagonism between modern liberal
ideas and the Catholic Church has grown rather
than decreased, to the point where many secular
thinkers regard religion (and especially the Catholic
religion) as the embodiment of bigotry; and
denounce Catholic schools as Madrassas of
indoctrination.

The new Mass, far from attracting vast crowds, has coincided with drastic falls in Mass attendance, to the point where some churches are closing, and some are muttering that we would have done better to keep everything as it was before the Council.

In this atmosphere it is not surprising that there is quite a bit of disillusion, even depression. And the gloomy mood is to be found not just in the pews but among priests, and even Bishops. Often it is only half noticed because when people are depressed they cannot describe their mood to themselves. But the effect of it all is to stifle initiative, reduce morale, and encourage a sense of helplessness. Let us be frank: in this country the Catholic Church has lost its self confidence, is floundering in a morass; it could barely be described in the words of the letter to the Hebrews as running in a race for the sake of the joy which is in the future.

But far from being discouraged this has ever been the story of Christianity. Even in those days after Pentecost, there was great disappointment when so many fellow countrymen of the apostles refused to believe the message. In the seventh century the sudden and rapid rise of Islam swept over the Middle East, virtually wiping out the main Christian Churches in Syria, Egypt and the Holy Land itself. Since the eighteenth century there have been repeated claims that Christianity has been disproved by Science: it is no more than a superstition. Again and again the Christian body has lived with apparent failure, but always it re-emerges with vigour and life. What happened after the second Vatican Council is what we should expect to happen with any major movement by the Church: confusion, disappointment, false euphoria that comes to nothing.

So the appeal of the Letter to the Hebrews is as

relevant today as it ever was. Keep faith, be ready to suffer (after all Christ did), fix your eyes on the future, *believe* that the Holy Spirit will guide us through. And we have one special encouragement that the Hebrew congregation did not have: we now stand with twenty centuries of Christian history to look back on. *We* can see that the church has survived one crisis after another, so we have every reason to suppose that it will emerge from our age with strength and vigour.

Homily given on 20th Sunday of Ordinary Time in year "C" at St. Aloysius' Glasgow.

Differences

God has different plans for different people.

"No one can come to me unless the Father allows him"
John 6:65

Unfortunately, you still meet people who do not believe in the Loch Ness Monster. My own personal encounter with the fabled beast took place as recently as this July, when I stayed for a night at the Youth Hostel on the North Shore of Loch Ness. The idyllic position of this Hostel with an enchanting view across the water at night time, more than compensated for the need, as is usual in Hostels, to sleep in a bunk-bed dormitory for around twelve people.

It was about 2am in that still, calm night that I woke up to a noise: this could only be the monster. A kind of rhythmic rattling growl alternating with a whistling sound like gas escaping. After a time one of the others got out of bed and woke the fiend, complaining that we could not sleep with the noise of his snoring. The poor man reacted with that strange innocence that befits snorers: he heard no sound, and was innocently enjoying a good night's sleep.

All this led me to reflect on the enormous divide in human affairs. Those who snore have no idea of the other world of those who can't sleep (the ones with the drawn haggard faces). The mutual antagonism between the two sides is fed by the utter incomprehension each has towards the other.

We see this in today's Gospel, where a chasm has

now appeared between those like Peter who have come to believe in Jesus, and those in the crowd who are disgusted by him: a division that was to deepen and consolidate to the point where some of his own people would reject our Lord, others would die for him.

There is a great tendency to become exasperated by such divisions. Somehow these unbelievers must be made to see that they are wrong, if need be by force. The history of Jews and Christians gives us some sad examples of attempts to coerce into unity.

But it is our Lord who tells us that some divisions are beyond human control: "No one can come to me, unless the Father allows him." We have to accept this, that Divine Providence grants faith to some and not to others; these others are doubtless provided for in God's plan, but not in ways known to us. What then is the Christian to do in the face of those who do not accept our belief?

We must accept the good faith of others.

We must not try to manipulate people into believing.

We must realise that it is God who rules the world, not us; and his plans may be beyond our comprehension.

The modern tendency is to attempt to solve these divides by claiming that they do not exist. To say politely that we all believe in the same God at heart, or that different religions boil down to the same thing. We do better to accept that there are real differences between Jew and Christian, between Christians and other religions, between believers and non-believers: they are painful differences and important; we cannot brush them aside. But at the same time we may believe that God in his incomprehensible way is providing for all sorts of different people, and we entrust those from whom we differ into his hands.

The attempt to quell the monster was not a great success: in time he went back to sleep, and the growls and hisses began all over again. However, I discovered it did have a kind of tuneful rhythm to it; not exactly Beethoven's 9th, but it had the effect in time of lulling me into sleep. There is room for everyone.

Homily given on 21st Sunday of Ordinary Time in year "B" at St. Aloysius' Glasgow.

Goodness

We want a good world, but we need a higher power to make it really good.

"For it is from within, from men's hearts, that evil intentions emerge"
Mark 7:21

The young man Augustine of Carthage fell under the influence of a sect called the Manichees. These believed, as many do today, that there are two competing forces in the world, a good one and a bad one. They also believed, as many do today, that the bad force operated through human beings: these were the ones who appeared to wreak destruction on the environment.

All the trouble in the world, it could be argued, comes from Homo Sapiens: pollution, devastation of forests, extermination of rare species – incredibly there would not even be mad cow disease if it were not for greedy entrepreneurs force-feeding the poor animals with a diet of mangled sheep's brains. Nature is pure and innocent: animals, plants, the landscape seem so harmless: but man somehow wrecks everything.

So Augustine fell under the spell of this Manichee religion, and of course it did him no good; for it is in essence a doctrine of despair. But painfully he eventually saw, that just as all creation is good, so must man as part of creation be potentially good, however much he may have drifted into evil; that good is what the world is all about because God who made it is good; evil is a perversion: it is not the plan.

However, let us, with Augustine, not lose sight

of the great evil that does seem to emanate from us; for he could see that we desperately need to be rescued from the state we are in, and cannot save ourselves. From the heart come all sorts of evils; only if a new Spirit is placed within us, will good influences emerge instead.

Those Pharisees and Scribes washing and sprinkling, cleansing and de-polluting so obsessively, were not entirely daft. They could see the evil that comes from us; the trouble is their solution was but a desperate pretence. Only Jesus the Redeemer can rescue us from the evil of our hearts, truly cleansing us, and giving us the wonderful privilege of becoming the crown of God's creation, not the destroyers of it.

Homily given on 22nd Sunday of Ordinary Time in year "B" at St. Aloysius' Glasgow.

Balanced Wisdom

Stonyhurst College in Lancashire is a
boarding and day school for boys and girls,
and has a small observatory in its grounds.

"The reasonings of mortals are unsure"
Wisdom 9:14

Among the many traditions of Stonyhurst is
Astronomy. We even have our own observatory, and
in the past Stonyhurst did some significant work on
observing the sun, analysing especially sun spots. In
more recent times the development of radio
telescopes, and now the placing of observation
platforms in orbit, away from clouds and ambient
light, has made it possible to penetrate ever more
deeply into space, and apprehend the sheer vastness
of our universe. It is sobering to think that earth is
but a speck of dust in the cosmos, drifting apparently
aimlessly through time.

The writer of the Book of Wisdom asks, "Who
can discover what is in the heavens?" yet he had a
much more simple concept of things than we do.
His understanding was that we are living in a vast
room, of which the ceiling is the blue sky, the stars
are little holes in the ceiling through which we see
specks of light, and the sun flits across the top of the
room each day like a butterfly. A nice, homely,
comfortably concept! At the same time the writer is
convinced that above the ceiling is another room,
the next floor, and here God, angels, heavenly spirits
all dwell in bliss and harmony. The trouble is that
there is no way of knowing what is going on up
there, unless perhaps one of the heavenly dwellers
discloses itself.

It is a simple view but it picks up on a vital point. There are some things we can learn by our own investigations. Science: physics, chemistry, biology, medical research; through these we are always finding out more and more about the universe in which we live. But there are other things that can only be known by us if they are revealed. We only know God, we only know why we are here on earth if it is told to us, from that other world.

And thus if we are to have a sound view of life, we need a discrete balance. On the one hand we must use our minds, we must research, learn to think critically, observe the world around us, assemble facts, marshal arguments: the whole purpose of education is to enable us to do this. But set against this we have to be humble enough to accept there are some things we cannot check for ourselves, matters which are only known if revealed to us, truths that the human intellect cannot attain unaided.

We do well to note that the writer of the Book of Wisdom is convinced that really vital knowledge is in the gift of God. He shows us truths we could never discover, discloses the true purpose of this vast universe, declares that the almost infinite reaches of stars and planets are not random, but have been created lovingly for us. He reveals that each of us has been personally formed over millions of years to live for a reason, and to have eternal life.

Homily given on 23rd Sunday of Ordinary Time in year "C" at Stonyhurst College, Lancs.

The Weak Kingdom

As the parable of the unforgiving steward indicates, in many ways the Church Jesus founded seems pathetic and weak.

"He cancelled the debt"
Matthew 18:27

The Chancellor of the exchequer cut a sorry sight: by now he should have gathered taxes totalling 10,000 gold talents (3 billion, 696 million pounds in today's money), and he has completely failed to do so. The chaos in the Kingdom with near anarchy, guerrillas in the hills, rival armed groups roaming the towns, has made tax collection a suicidal occupation. The king knows in his heart of hearts he will not get his money: if he presses for it he may well lose his crown as well as his revenue; so with a certain astuteness he decides to make a virtue of necessity. He will pose as a generous, understanding ruler, make a great show of forgiving the Chancellor, get the message abroad to citizens and peasantry that they will not have to pay their dues. Maybe the pay-off will be some popularity for himself: maybe the people will prefer him, an ineffective but harmless old buffer, to the cut throat guerrillas who are trying to wrest the kingdom from him.

Of course it will mean a dim future: a feeble ruler supported by ineffective officials; hardly the iron fisted muscle of the neighbouring kingdoms. But it is the only way. What is more it might work! Perhaps the people will be loyal out of pity rather than fear, perhaps they will grow to love this king who is so much one of them; sharing the peasant anxiety about debts, the fear of oppression, the constant humiliations from the great and powerful. A king like that is someone you can feel for.

Now I regret to inform you that it is this pitiful set-up to which you and I belong: the kingdom of heaven, or the church, is founded on bankruptcy. God, to whom we owe huge sums, knows this and has abandoned his rights: he will just accept us, destitute as we are, providing we will form a community on this basis. None of us need repay our debts; the snag is none of us can reclaim what is due to us either.

Let us accept our dubious privilege: there is a place for us in this heavenly set-up however much we have failed, regardless of the fact that we have no right to be here, in spite of being unworthy of our position, and not having contributed our share to it. But this new kingdom being founded on love rather than on compulsion compels us to accept all the other second rate backsliders who surround us. We can stay for nothing, on condition that everyone else can do so too. It is a new system: but it will work. It has been inaugurated from heaven: it is the only way we will be able to live with God and with each other.

Homily given on 24th Sunday of Ordinary time in year "A" at St. Aloysius' Glasgow.

Power v. Power

There is a sharp contrast between the power of God's Kingdom, and the power of money.

"You cannot be the slave both of God and of money"
Luke 16:13

Visitors to Kali's temple get a surprise: in spite of being the most important religious centre of Bengal, the shrine is only a small dirty dungeon-like cellar of a place, crammed with sweating bodies squeezing into the space to worship the idol, a bedlam of noise, of bells and incantations. The actual idol makes one want to laugh – although it would be very unwise to do so. It is a kind of doll: a black mask on a cushion, hollow and grotesque: from the face a long tongue hangs out indicating not a thirst for milk (as with some idols apparently) but blood; a point emphasised by the necklace of skulls.

Calcutta, Kalighat, or Kali's steps, is named after the temple of Kali. You get things from Kali if you pay for them: she requires sacrifices from her devotees as the condition of granting her favours. A business-like practical arrangement that well suits the ambitious down-to-earth Bengali mentality. We in the West would sneer at all this worship of idols; but this is because we do not understand it. The hollow black mask does not do anything: it only symbolises the state of affairs that comes about when people make a God of dominance, power and lust. For the sacrifice which is demanded to achieve this is in human blood. If for a moment you would care to picture an atom bomb or a tank with a mask painted on it, tongue hanging out, and garlanded with skulls, you may begin to realise that it is not only Bengalis who worship Kali. By and large we in the West want power, dominance and wealth: these favours are only granted for a price.

Pretty well all temples in India have a hostel attached to them where pilgrims and devotees can stay whilst on a visit; and the temple of Kali is no exception. But the hostel at Kalighat fell into disuse, and eventually was given to Mother Teresa as a home for the dying. The visitor to this home, right next to Kalighat, will get quite the opposite feeling from the one he got on going to the Temple next door. An air of peace and calm, on a mantle-piece a picture of Jesus with a message "Jesus welcomes us to his Father's house" or such like.

Let us consider for a moment the puzzling nature of this home for the dying. After all, one might well say that for Jesus to welcome a person into his Father's house, by having them brought in there to die, is not much use. Mother Teresa and her sisters go round Calcutta picking up dying people, abandoned infants and so forth, and take them to this home where they die. What does that achieve? It would seem that to love is not very useful; it is to give not to invest; it doesn't achieve much. Mother Teresa and her sisters are loving people; not looking for a return. If you want to get things done you have to go next door: Kali gets things done – for a price.

And so two places, next door to each other, but worlds apart. The one so forceful, down-to-earth, practical, realistic: the home of ruthlessness. The other soft and impractical, uncalculating, living off sentiment: the dwelling of Holy Spirit. You have to choose: love or money; God or Mammon; giving or grabbing. The two will not mix.

Homily given on 25th Sunday of Ordinary Time in year "C" at Saints Peter & Paul Mitcham.

Caring

The 'Arrupe programme' is a course of social service done by school pupils.

"Between us and you, a great gulf has been fixed"
Luke 16:26

George Orwell of 1984 fame decided to try what life was like as a tramp. Nervously he signed in at a doss house, and there as he entered the hot, stuffy room with all the down and outs crowded together he thought his worst fears were about to be realised. A bulky stevedore, shoved towards him, arms flailing, face contorted. This would be it, the inevitable fight, the hatred these men must feel for an Eton educated toff like Orwell. But as the man, obviously half drunk, got near him, he simply called out, "'ave a cup of tea, mate" and grinned. It struck Orwell straight away that this wretch was simply a human being.

The rich man in the parable, never tried to find out what the poor man was like, he just remained cocooned in his feasts, his purple linen, his party friends. He was not as such a bad man, but his riches wrapped him up in a world of his own.

Most people who yearn for wealth never notice how it cuts them off from humanity. Does it occur to those people who live in gated estates, with security guards to protect them, high walls to surround them; does it ever dawn on them, that they are imprisoning themselves, shutting themselves off, isolating themselves from real men and women? The rich live under a great illusion that they have it all; in reality they have nothing. Or at least they only have things in place of spirit, things instead of humanity, things rather than soul.

Thus in time the rich man in the Gospel finds himself utterly isolated, thirsting desperately for any human contact. He sees the poor man in a world of shared souls, in the heart of Abraham, and earnestly yearns for human contact, even with the pathetic Lazarus. But sadly, Abraham explains, it is too late: he has chained himself up in his wealth, erected a great wall (no doubt for security) between himself and real people. It is no longer possible to make heart to heart contact; he must remain tormented in his consuming wealth.

The poor, like Lazarus, are held up to us as models in the Scriptures because they are real human beings; they have nothing except themselves; like Job they can declare "naked I came from my mother's womb, naked I shall return." It is like the so-called good thief and Jesus tied to their crosses: there was nothing separating them, one is God incarnate, the other a robber, but they are their true selves, they can communicate, they can be deeply human even in their wretched state. But the rich bury their humanity in posh clothes, fast cars, sleek yachts, gated estates: in time these things destroy the soul.

In this college we are making strong efforts to mix with true humanity: in the Arrupe programme, going out to diverse people with genuine needs; in the projects with St Peter's Kubatana and St Paul's Musami. But let us not blithely assume that we are going to solve the problems of the poor: the truth is that these people in need will show us what it is to be human.

Homily given on 26th Sunday of Ordinary Time in year "C" at Stonyhurst College, Lancs.

Family

We can only be human as social beings.
It is as communities that we flourish.

"It is not good that the man should be alone"
Genesis 2:18

Years ago the received wisdom was that everything is made up of atoms, perceived as basic bricks with which everything was bound together. Every atom was thought to be absolutely solid, like a nut or a brick, and splitting the atom was meant to be the great aim, maybe the impossible dream of science. How things have changed! Now we have come to learn that what was called an atom is in reality a complex of electrons, protons, neutrons and whatever, all whizzing around each other, like bees in a beehive. But of course what was true all along is that the atom, however complex, keeps its unity, and, though so tiny, continues to be the basic building block of the entire universe.

When God created the first human, it seemed it did not quite work. True this creature had intelligence and life, was able to rule over all animals and plants, and with royal condescension knighted each animal with a name. But human had no equal, no one with whom to share life; like a dense atom each human was alone.

And so the Lord took a momentous decision. After all, the divine Trinity is a-buzz with activity with Father, Son and Holy Spirit interacting, sharing, living and loving at the speed of light. Why not give the human an inner life like that? And so that human atom God had created was transformed into an interacting life, into male and female. God did not create man, and then create woman. He created humanity and made man and woman the interacting parts: living by each other, with each other, through each other. Just as God is not God independently of Father Son and Holy Spirit, so we are only human in sharing with each other, male and female.

At the Labour Party conference last week there was recognition of the vital importance of the family if we are to have a fulfilled and happy society. So true. Though so tiny, it is the family which is the atom of society; having a strong unity and a highly developed internal life. We must strive to support all family life, and recognise its sublime imitation of the communal life of God.

It is not good for man to be alone. The Holy Trinity is not alone. Our families provide that vital community from which human life can flourish.

Homily given on 27th Sunday of Ordinary Time in year "B" at St. Aloysius' Glasgow.

The Reluctant Disciple

There is a lot to be said for the half-hearted Christian!

"He noticed a man who was not wearing a wedding garment"
Matthew 22:12

Are you one of those people who arrives late, leaves early, shows little interest; mutters the responses inaudibly, does not join in hymns? Are you a reluctant Catholic? Well, you have not given up altogether; you do come to Mass in some minimal way; perhaps it is quite an effort to do that. Enormous numbers have made their excuses and left: you are here however unwillingly.

Observe that you fit the profile of the guests at the wedding feast. They did not want to come, they were pressured into it: perhaps felt out of place, embarrassed, in strange company. Part of the feeling those compelled guests must have had was "we do not really belong here". So it turns out that the reluctant Catholic is the normal one! And let it be said that it is often people who do not have much enthusiasm who have a solid faith. They have realised the Jesus way is not a hobby, but a sober commitment; they have noticed that it will entail the cross, suffering, the sacrifice of much that others can have: so perhaps they have a down-to-earth faith, one that has noticed the cost of believing.

But, and this is important, our faith cannot stand still. It will, over a period, either weaken and die away, or it will strengthen and flourish. The guests at the wedding feast were press-ganged into attending, but they knew that to stay they must adjust their lives at least to the extent of wearing the right clothes. The one who did not wear a wedding garment doubtless noticed that there was an implication in this whole business: the king who begins by taking anybody into the hall, then requires that they pose as real wedding guests, next he will be wanting them to swear loyalty to his newly married son, eventually to take up arms in his cause. We start by simply being here, but we must progress to belonging here.

So ask yourself, "How do I come to belong at this wedding? How do I make it my home?"

First, do not excuse yourself with claims to be but an ordinary, simple Christian. You have been chosen; God's grace is to work in you; your weaknesses are not a problem for the redeeming power of Jesus: do not do yourself down.

Second, find something about the way you live your religion that does enter your heart. Perhaps you find it helpful to pray; perhaps you like silence; maybe you read the bible, or use a prayer book; perhaps you get on well with certain priests, or like a particular church. Build on these.

Third, choose to accept God's grace. The first guests refused to come; the people from the highways and byways did not chose to come; but by wearing a wedding garment they chose to stay. You cannot be a Christian except by accepting the way of Jesus Christ in opposition to the ways of the world around you.

Homily given on 28th Sunday of Ordinary Time in year "A" at St. Aloysius' Glasgow.

True Coin

The village of Flash lies at 500metres
(1,640 feet) above sea level in Staffordshire,
9km south-west of Buxton.

"Give back to God what belongs to God"
Matthew 22:21

On a walking holiday you sometimes come across
some extraordinary things. In September I unknow-
ingly arrived at a village which was both odd and
famous. First of all a notice on a wall proclaimed
"This post office is the highest in England"; then it
turned out that there was no post office – it had
closed; but most intriguing of all was the name of
the village, a name that understandably was not
greatly publicised, the highest village in England is
actually called "Flash".

In the pub I resisted asking the inevitable
question, "What do you call a man from Flash?" But
I soon learnt that this village had given its name to
the English language. For it turned out that it was
once famous as the centre for producing forged
currency. Taking advantage of its high and remote
location the inhabitants developed a very profitable
line in producing counterfeit notes: so the expression
a "flash note", not much used today, means a forged
one.

Nowadays of course thanks to high quality
photocopiers it is all to easy to produce good quality
forgeries. It seems that at any given moment there
are £17,000,000 worth of forged "readies" in circu-
lation. Some of you here may have had the very
unpleasant experience of getting one by accident,
and finding it quite worthless.

Obviously no government wants to see its

currency debased: a dubious currency both undermines trade and reflects badly on the government itself. And in the ancient world the emperor would prove his good faith by issuing currency only in precious metals (gold and silver) and stamping his image upon each coin. When a person paid taxes they were acknowledging the immense benefit that came from the emperor's treasury, and acknowledging the special ownership he could claim on the coins he had issued.

But Jesus seems to have known a bit more about currency than the Pharisees who tried to trap him. He was aware of other coin; coin that had originally been issued with a more exalted image stamped on it, and of purer metal than even the emperor could obtain. The coin is any man or woman, the image on it is God's image, stamped at the moment of creation when God said "Let us make man in our own image and likeness".

Such coins should be totally reliable; their origin patently evident. But what in fact has happened? We have debased and altered what came from the Mint: the image seems to have got rubbed off, and the original metal has got terribly mixed in with stuff of very doubtful origin, so much so that the Pharisees, as perhaps ourselves, are no longer aware of where we originated, or to whom we rightly belong. Small wonder that we do not think to whom it should be returned.

Jesus is asking us to pay the real tax, ourselves; to the original issuer, God. Though we know that the coin has now become "flash money" he will help us to purify it and restore the original image, so that we can give back to God what truly belongs to him.

Homily given on 29th Sunday of Ordinary Time in year "A" at Saints Peter & Paul's, Mitcham.

The Conqueror

We can 'conquer' others by serving them.

"Anyone who wants to be great among you, must be servant of all"
Mark 10:33

> 'Some talk of Alexander and some of Hercules, of Hector and Lysander and such great men as these.'

Indeed they do, but such people would have been even more greatly talked about in the first century. For that was the age that looked back on wave after wave of world conquest. Sennacherib of Assyria rampaged throughout the Middle East, 700 BC; Alexander the Great conquered his native Greece, then Turkey, Persia, Syria, Israel, even pushed through the Khyber pass into India, 300 BC; 63 BC in about the time that Julius Caesar was conquering France, and even raiding these shores, his rival Pompey established Roman rule in Israel, and even colonised Egypt.

Yes, if it is world conquest you are interested in; the people of Jesus' time could have told you of many such.

But then there arose a man who was to be the greatest conqueror of them all. He would have no army; no weapons; he relied on a strategy that has never been thought of before or since. A strategy that sounds crazy, perhaps is crazy, but has one huge advantage: it works. His method was simple. Instead of trying to dominate people, rather than prove yourself strong and threatening; you must actually aim to serve them.

It is an astonishing notion; would have meant nothing to Sennacherib, Alexander, Caesar, Pompey. It seemed very odd to James and John who had their own ideas. But it did conquer the world, and not just in the flash in a pan style of Alexander, but permanently.

You may say you are not actually intending to conquer the world. Glad to hear it. But the Jesus formula: "The one who would be great among you, must be the servant of all", will work locally as much as globally; as effective in a house as it is in a continent. In all our relationships – family, partner, people at work, people we meet – we constantly have the option: do I try to dominate or do I try to serve? If you want relationships to last; then use the Jesus formula: it works on every level.

Homily given on 30th Sunday of Ordinary Time in year "B" at Stonyhurst College, Lancs.

A Heart Healed

The miracles of Jesus includes ones where he cures hearts and minds.

"Today salvation has come to this house"
Source

One of the slightly bizarre items in the extensive Stonyhurst Collection of Historical Items is the skull of Cardinal Morton. Cardinal Morton was a sort of Chancellor of the Exchequer to Heny VII, a Gordon Brown of the fifteenth century. Henry VII had great success in reforming the treasury, and in getting a proper taxation system in place, and Morton is credited with being his chief agent in this. It is claimed he used to carry a small fork around with which he would prod Barons, demanding they pay up: whether the expression to "fork out" comes from this, I leave to your own imagination.

What is obvious, is that Morton would not have been too popular with the Barons. So too with Zacchaeus; he climbs a tree not merely because he is short, but more because the crowd "make it impossible" for him to approach Jesus. Zacchaeus was rich, but doubtless very lonely. Not only was he forcing his countrymen to give over their money, he was collaborating with the hated Romans, betraying his religion and nation.

But Jesus came to help the ostracised: the lepers, the cripples, yes, and even the filthy rich. He was ready to accept this outcast and welcome him, and it was this that moved Zacchaeus to change his whole way of life. From extortionist he becomes a lovable, caring and generous man; all in a few minutes. And his change of heart starts from a kind of curiosity: he wants to see Jesus, climbs a tree to get a view, and Jesus spots him.

So Jesus gives Zacchaeus a chance to be included: "I must stay at your house today"; and Zacchaeus, realises this is code for "Accept me and my ways, and I will give you a new life". Zacchaeus realises he has a bargain, welcomes Jesus, and changes his life there and then.

It is a wonderful example of a spiritual miracle of Jesus; one where he changes a person's heart. The physical miracles are dramatic, but surely the spiritual ones are more important. In our age when we hope that science and medicine may achieve miracle cures on our bodies, we are still as helpless as ever for cures to our character. Jesus shows he has the power to change the heart of Zacchaeus: how marvellous if he did the same for us.

For probably each person here wants to be, in some respects a different person; wants to be able to enter into the hearts of others: with generosity, caring, forgiveness; but is held back, as Zacchaeus once was, by those barriers we erect by our rivalry and self-seeking. Jesus shows us that if we put faith in him, which means responding with generosity and sincerity, he can make us new persons: from lonely self-seekers, to warm hearted, fulfilled men and women.

Homily given on 31st Sunday of Ordinary Time in year "C" at Stonyhurst College, Lancs.

Higher Life

The Sadducees are asking which of seven husbands a woman will have in the next life, given that she was married to all seven in this one.

"He is God of the living"
Luke 20:38

When Charles Darwin published his famous book, The Origin of Species, it caused a great shock to most of the Christian world. People assumed that God had created each kind of creature fixed in its nature, rather as a given model of car remains according to its design as long as it lasts. The idea that creatures may change and evolve, seemed to suggest that God had not done his job properly, and the notion that human beings had arisen from the animal world, seemed almost blasphemous.

The Sadducees of today's Gospel thought along the same lines. God had made the world as it is, and that was that. If they ever considered an after life they conceived it as a repeat of the present pattern; just as a person with an old car might be able to do a major repair, and then run it again for a number of years. They could not perceive Resurrection as change, any more than those Christians who were shocked by Darwin could see life as evolving.

But God does not make creatures in the way that Henry Ford made the model T car. God is Life, so what he creates desires to Live. And thus, in so far as an organism has only a weak life, it will strive for all its worth to attain a higher life, to get to a state where it can live more, live better, live longer: but live! What is more, to achieve a higher form of life change is needed: we must adapt to environments, seize opportunities to grow, be prepared to undergo a revolution if it will give us a future. And all this because God created things to live, for God is pure life.

So our Lord confronts the Sadducees, as if he was Charles Darwin. We do not merely live, we change in order to live: we were created to develop to fulfilment, we are to be "the same as the angels". And the biggest change we will undergo is the Resurrection, when we will make that crucial evolution to a state where our bodies are spiritualised – able to live eternally, capable of total fulfilment; attaining their purpose: to live as God lives.

Homily given on 32nd Sunday of Ordinary Time in year "C" at Stonyhurst College.

Out of Time

In a puzzling way we live in time, even though time has come to an end!

"Before this generation has passed away, all these things will have taken place"
Mark 13:30

Even in the first century Christians were puzzled about the return of Christ and the end of the world. He said it would all happen in their lifetime, but we still seem to be waiting. Hence it is that many of us feel puzzled and empty as we listen to those strange passages that talk of the moon failing, the world ending and Christ returning.

Perhaps we can get some understanding if we imagine a sort of double time. Let me illustrate this with a true story:

A certain Father Gerhard Pieper, a Jesuit originating from East Germany, went to work in the Missions in Rhodesia as it was then, now Zimbabwe. All Jesuits do a final course called the Tertianship, and Fr Gerhard broke off from his mission and went to Australia to do this. The Tertianship includes a number of pastoral experiences, so in Australia he went and worked in a parish for three months. He proved to be quite popular, and it was arranged that when he got back to Rhodesia he would send monthly letters telling them about his work on the Mission.

The civil war was raging at that time in Rhodesia, and one day the parish heard that Fr Gerhard had been killed: he had been stopped on his motorbike and massacred. About two weeks later his usual letter arrived, full of chirpy comments, plans for the work, news of activities, etc. You can imagine the peculiar feeling it induced in the church that Sunday when the people heard read a letter from someone whom they knew to be dead.

This in miniature is the whole Christian story. The world as it used to be has ended, Jesus has left it and gone elsewhere. We live in the world, but as strangers who don't quite belong, or as in a dream where things seem real, but one day we will wake up and see ourselves truly, and realise that life was in many ways unreal.

Understanding this is important because the Christian needs to be in the world as a stranger; we belong elsewhere. Our values, our hopes, our expectations focus on a different sphere. A large part of our task is to work out how to live in this world.

Homily given on 33rd Sunday of Ordinary Time in year "B" at Saints Peter and Paul, Mitcham.

No Ruin

Since Jesus has had such a huge effect on the history of the world, we should ask where he has left his mark.

"So, you are a king then?"
John 18:37

Any king worth his salt will leave his mark on the country he governed. Take Herod the Great. He may have been a bad man, but there is no doubt he was a king: the numerous buildings he left behind him are witness to that – the temple in Jerusalem which he rebuilt, the fortress at Masada, the town of Caesarea. It is almost as though Herod was saying "You will not forget me in a hurry."

In contrast to this Jesus, who claimed to be a King, left nothing behind him; he did not even leave a book to record his teaching: in one sense he vanishes from history because he left nothing.

And yet this is not quite true. Jesus built up a group of supporters in whom he left his mark: these became imbued with his teaching and passed it on to others. Whilst there is no ruin to commemorate Jesus, his followers are his memorial: a living, growing, expanding body.

Then there is a more important reason why we have no monument to mark his passing. It is the simple but crucial one that he is not a past king! As Jesus stands before Pilate that day it seems that his kingly claims are coming to a dreadful end: in fact he is about to begin his reign. He will rise from the dead, ascend to heaven and be given sovereignty over all peoples; at the end of time he will come to judge them.

But where does that leave us? Jesus is reigning, but invisibly. He does not impose his reign: there are no armies, no fortresses, no bank issuing his currency. He reigns through the heart, with your consent. You can ignore his kingship; no police force will enforce it.

And if you do accept his reign, it will make its mark: not leaving some ruin for archaeologists to examine. No! its mark will be on your character: you will come to show the imprint of him in your actions, attitudes, reactions. You will both be the citizens of his kingdom and the very temple that marks it.

Homily given on Christ the King Sunday of year "B" at St. Aloysius' Glasgow.

Be Prepared!

We need to try to look forwards, even though it is unnerving.

"What I say to you, I say to all 'stay awake!'"
Mark 13:37

Many are the attempts that have been made to understand dreams, from the Prophet Daniel to the Psychiatrist Sigmund Freud. In all the searching for the meaning, a simple point is often overlooked, that there are really two types of dream, pleasant ones and nightmares; and characteristic of them is that pleasant dreams look back over familiar ground; whilst nightmares face forward into the terrifying unknown.

In general when we look at the past, we feel easy about it; for the past is now finished, happened, all over; even if it was a disaster at the time. Like the day when, like Sir Walter Raleigh, you threw your coat over a muddy puddle for a lady, except that the coat landed with a splash that went all over her dress: now that your faux pas is all past it can be looked at with a glow of nostalgia, seen as a joke.

But the future is always about what might happen, and who knows? Will there be an accident in the family? Might I become redundant? Can I get through that exam next summer? All our worries focus on what may come, and a nightmare is a blown up dramatisation of our darkest fears.

Christians often avoid (perhaps they want to avoid), those teachings of Jesus when he speaks about things to come – teachings, called apocalyptic, which are rather like a nightmare: devastation of Jerusalem, earthquakes, famine, end of the world; all happening in a chaotic jumble. Indeed it is notable that this season of Advent (which means coming) is turned by us into PostVent: looking back 2,000 years to what happened long ago, and making it as glowing and reassuring as possible.

But the point of Ad-vent will be largely lost unless we make it a time for getting ready to meet our Lord in the future. If we look to the future, we will be able to face the future, like St Stephen the martyr who as he was dying looked up to heaven and saw Christ sitting at the right hand of God. Christians really have something to look forward to: we are getting ready to meet Christ; we are confident he is drawing us towards our eternal enduring home; we are going somewhere; we are pilgrims on a journey, let's fix our minds on our destination.

Homily given on 1st Sunday of Advent in year "B" at St. Aloysius' Glasgow.

Difficult Christmas

Christmas is still good news for those who
find it a depressing time.

"Console my people, console them"
Isaiah 40:1

The prophet Isaiah lived at a time when Israel was
increasingly drifting away from religion: trade, wealth
and prosperity were replacing the need for God.
One can almost see him in Jerusalem, arguing in the
Bazaar about keeping the Sabbath, and being told
that the market requires stalls to open on the Sabbath,
and people want it anyway!

The great conviction of this noble prophet was
man's need of God. His country, Israel, was only
about the size of Wales, squashed between mighty
Egypt on the one hand, and aggressive Assyria on
the other. To trust in wealth, to rely on political
alliances, to bank on the strength of the army – these
were simply illusions. Only God could save Israel,
but Israel in its arrogance had turned from God.

Isaiah had had an intense vision: in the temple
in Jerusalem he had actually seen God, God in glory
surrounded by angels. It had frightened him, but it
had deeply moved him: he went around convinced
of the presence of God in the midst of the city, and
was profoundly disturbed at the failure of the leaders
of the people to appreciate what was there.

To Isaiah there were two great truths: man is
puny and feeble; God is glorious and great. The
pretension of Israel in relying on its own strength
was but a pathetic illusion. Only God could protect
the nation.

People who go to church can be divided into

two classes: those who believe in God and those who don't! Or more precisely those who rely on God and those who rely on themselves. For is it not true that we often "believe" in God only in the sense that we vaguely suppose there is some remote figure existing in space who does not affect us? May it be the case that when the chips are down we are hoping that our self-confidence, our sense of our own importance, some sense of the power of science, or the provisions of the government, are going to see us through life? Do we really think that our only hope is in God?

Now notice carefully to whom that reading from Isaiah was directed. It is the broken hearted, the ones who have come to realise their hopes were vain, who now know that they must be helped by a power beyond themselves: it is to them that the good news comes.

The coming of Christ at Christmas is, then, particularly for those who do feel overwhelmed by life. Contrary to popular pretence Christmas can for many be a difficult time: of memories of what once was, but is no more, of hopes that collapsed and dreams that were shattered. If you are one of those, see Christmas as a time of grace, because if you come to believe that on God alone can you rely, you will have discovered a very profound truth: one which Isaiah recognised and proclaimed 2,600 years ago.

Homily given on 2nd Sunday of Advent in year "B" at St. Aloysius' Glasgow.

Going Nowhere

We need to make a spiritual journey.

"He will prepare your way before you"
Matthew 11:10 (from Malachi 3:1)

John the Baptist's talk of filling valleys and carving through mountains is all too familiar to us, as we see the English countryside submerge under the ever expanding network of motorways, bypasses, cloverleaf junctions.

If you stand on a bridge over a motorway, it is easy to feel that the whole hectic business is pointless. As one set of vehicles hurtles like mad towards Birmingham, another set of traffic is speeding frantically in the opposite direction! Is anybody going anywhere? Perhaps that car racing north is going from nowhere to nowhere else. Will the person who zips frenetically from A to B be in the least bit different in B from what they were in A? We are all rushing to get to a place, yet we are not a whit different when we arrive.

What John the Baptist wanted when he said "Prepare a Way for the Lord" was for us to clear a path into our hearts: that is where we have placed obstacles, twists and turns, hills and ditches to obstruct the Lord, to prevent him from getting through to us. And this is why we never change in spite of rushing up and down motorways so much. Only God can change us, but we have blocked every access to our hearts.

We do not have to do much: just give our Lord a way in; He will make us new. But He must be able to find a road into our hearts, else nothing can be done.

So how do we clear a path, and make a real difference in our lives? Here is one suggestion: think how much it would affect you if your family prayed together as a family! Of course this is difficult nowadays when families do not do a lot together. But there must be some opportunity: what about saying grace before Christmas dinner? Or sing a carol together around the Christmas tree? Or saying some night prayers as a family on Christmas Eve? You would all need to agree beforehand that this is what you are going to do. But if you do this you will find that you have in a few minutes travelled a much greater distance than you ever go on a motorway.

Homily given on 3rd Sunday of Advent in year "A"
at St. Aloysius' Glasgow.

Faith and Courage

Mary had faith and courage.

"Let what you have said be done to me"
Luke 1:38

It has been claimed that the male of the species is characterised by an adventurous outgoing temperament, whilst the female is supposedly docile and home loving. Thus in the rather dubious portrayals of our cave dwelling forebears, we are often shown pictures of men in skins charging through their Jurassic parks to spear ferocious animals, whilst the women just sit outside the cave cooking the meals. The implication is that courage is the sphere of man, caution the domain of woman.

Our knowledge of what went on in caves is largely based on our knowledge of what we would expect to have happened in them: in short it is imaginary! But our knowledge of the birth of Jesus originates from a fairly carefully researched description by a competent historian, St Luke.

And as Luke begins his story with a man whose courage failed him: Zechariah when promised a son, falters: "how can I be sure?" is his question; so he continues it with a woman who trusts: boldly but quietly she accepts the invitation to a great adventure; the adventure of believing; she permits the Lord to launch her on to a life of change and challenge.

Mary in her life will not be domestically looking after the home: time and again she ventures out on expeditions with great courage and boldness. Indeed straight after the angel's message she is off to Judea to see and help her cousin Elizabeth; her pregnancy will be born to term in a journey to a distant stable;

with her child and Joseph she will become a refugee; she is the one who is not at home on Good Friday but at the foot of the cross; and it is Mary who is to be found as the heart of the first disciples in the upper room waiting for the Holy Spirit.

By her fearless dedication to God's plan Mary achieves what so many of us seek: self fulfilment. What life was ever richer than hers? Who could have realised their potential as well as she did? What person possessed herself in greater freedom than she? Mistakenly, people think that freedom is doing your own thing; yet this ends up as doing nothing very much! No, we are free when we launch our lives into the ocean of God's great design; for in truth God's plan for the world is for the fulfilment of our deep human longing.

In this final Sunday before Christmas, let us be inspired by the bold woman who said yes to God: in this she said yes to Jesus, yes to herself, yes to human destiny.

Homily given on 4th Sunday of Advent in year "C"
at St. Aloysius' Glasgow.

Closeness Counts

Coming into contact with Jesus has a deep effect on us.

"They found the baby lying in the manger"
Luke 2:16

When the Hebrews were slaves in Egypt, and the Pharaoh strove to exterminate them, decreeing that all male children should be killed at birth, a woman who bore a baby boy hid him for three months; then in desperation, unable to conceal her child any longer she made a wicker basket, covered it with pitch and left him floating on the river Nile.

Pharaoh's daughter coming to bathe in the river found the child among the reeds, and hearing him crying she was moved with pity and adopted the child herself. From the very family which was set upon exterminating the Hebrews, one ended up nourishing its future leader in the Royal Palace, and all because of a simple human sentiment of pity. The hostility of Egyptian and Hebrew quietly melted at the power of a tiny child to move a human heart. King Pharaoh considered the Hebrews a menace, a danger, a threat; but to Pharaoh's daughter the little Hebrew baby was pitiable and appealing.

To those who actually found Jesus out in the fields lying in a manger — the shepherds, Mary, Joseph, the wise men — the child was charmingly innocent, attractive and gentle, quiet and peaceful. But there were others — Herod and his court — who only knew dark rumours: a new potentate born, a usurper, a threat to their position. These people were in time to engineer the death of Jesus.

And thus it came about that as Pharaoh on the

one hand feared and hated Moses, whilst his daughter on the other pitied and rescued him; so some were to befriend and trust Jesus, whilst others would scheme his crucifixion. No human being can avoid going one way or the other.

The secret is to find Jesus. Those who get near him, like him; those who discover a helpless child find divine power; those who see peace in the manger, find peace in their hearts. You cannot get really close to Jesus without his heavenly influence entering your heart: perhaps that is why God became a child, because we would naturally love a child, and before we realised, would find ourselves loving God.

Jesus, born today, offers us friendship, love and peace from God: his very weakness in a manger is a sign that God has not come to threaten, but to befriend us. If we will embrace Jesus his good influence will permeate our souls: like Pharaoh's daughter we will come to love the one whom others blindly hate.

Homily given at Christmas Day Dawn Mass
at St. Aloysius' Glasgow.

Lost and Found

Perhaps our modern technology misses the point.

"We have seen his star as it arose"
Matthew 2:2

"At least I know how to get there", thought Carlton-Browne, as the three of them rode across the sandy waste. "As for this Indian, and the Arab, they obviously haven't much clue. The Indian, so excitable, no stiff upper lip, with his constant chirping of 'The stars are most auspicious.' The Arab, on the other hand, morose and solemn; none of that sense of humour that gets we British through every adversity. He simply pronounces fatalistically 'It has been written.'" "Still", Carlton-Browne's thoughts continued, "with me to lead them, we should get there alright."

Carlton-Browne, it should be said, regarded himself as an intrepid explorer. But not only did he have his self confidence and sense of effortless superiority to help him, C-B was equipped with the very latest in electronic aids. Lap Top running at 13-giga-hertz, mobile phone on his belt, state of the art Global Positioning monitor. As it happened he was having trouble booting the Lap Top, thanks to the bucking and staggering of this infernal camel; his mobile seemed to have hit a shadow, as he could not get a signal at the moment. But not to worry, the Global Positioning System would give his location quite simply anywhere on earth; indeed it was so state of the art that it had also been programmed to give accurate locations on the moon, in anticipation of the day when explorers like Carlton-Browne would be wandering across its surface. Another feature of this extraordinary gizmo was the green button, which when pressed gave instructions on the way to go to get to a chosen destination.

Unfortunately, things weren't working quite as anticipated. Our hero had been quite encouraged when their tracks joined with some others already printed in the sand: clearly some people had already found the route, now it was a case of simply trailing them. But after a time it dawned on Carlton-Browne that they were following the tracks of precisely three camels, and the truth of the situation began to sink in. Annoyingly, the other two did not seem in the least bothered: the Indian chirped "The stars are most auspicious", the Arab stuck to his monotonous "It has been written." He pressed the green button on the GPS: it came back with a strange message – it just said: "Go home!"

The shack that eventually appeared on the plain did not seem much to Carlton B., but the others were content to head for it. "Maybe it will do for an overnight rest", he thought. When they got there it turned out to contain a new born baby with his mother and father, there were some shepherds too, and a number of farm animals. At first he could not make out what the strange feeling was that entered him: the place seemed so very ordinary, and yet also felt very special. Then as he looked round at the others he began to notice one thing they all had in common: all of them, even the animals seemed to be at home there; it was as though this was where they belonged. Just as a pigeon's homing instinct will take it back to its roost, so it seemed all these in the stable had come home; come to where they belonged; come to where they had started from. They had not only found this child; they had found themselves.

They had not only found their destination, they had found their origin. Now that they had got there, they had arrived at where they had started from. And the child seemed to show all this: he was just beginning life, but somehow Browne felt that he, and the others, had found their beginning. A sense of peace spread over him, because all that searching, exploring, discovering now seemed to miss the point: it was himself he needed to find, and this child showed him himself. At last, instead of endlessly trying to work out where he was going, he was getting a feel for where he came from. In this shack he was at home: he did not need to find the way any more.

As they left the small homestead, Carlton-Browne barely noticed that he had left behind his Lap Top, his mobile, even the Global Positioning monitor.

Homily given at Midnight Mass in St. Aloysius' Glasgow.

Mirrors

Jesus can be thought of as a mirror that shows us who we are.

"The Word was the true light who enlightens everyone"
John 1:9

Only in fairy tales do princesses risk looking in mirrors and asking "who is the fairest of them all?" For most of us an encounter with a mirror, often early in the morning, reveals a haggard stranger, bags under the bloodshot eyes, staring stupidly out in our direction: we go away wondering who could look so dreadful, and hope that we do not meet the apparition again.

The awkward thing about a mirror is that it tells the truth – best avoided. A great deal of our energy goes into striving to disguise who we really are, not merely from other people, no, rather from ourselves. Of course it maybe that if we were to risk a proper look we would find we are not really as ghastly as we suppose: but it takes courage to do that and we shy off.

What a challenge it would be if there was a live, walking, talking questioning mirror about. One which would search you, make you face yourself, delve into the depths of your heart. The Ancient Philosopher, Socrates, got into trouble and was forced to commit suicide, because he went round Athens challenging people to confront themselves, to face up to what they are. His great motto "know yourself" sounds excellent: we avoid it like the plague!

The real you, the real me, I say this seriously, is

Jesus Christ. Know him and you know yourself; look at him and you are looking at yourself: all the wonder of human nature created as the temple of God; all the goodness of divine love; all the wisdom, science, intelligence, foresight of the heavenly creator – they are in Jesus Christ, they are in you. We have lost our true selves, muddied them with sin, and so "he comes to his own, and we, his own, will not receive him". But the fact is that the Word joins himself utterly with our human nature, and thus joins our human nature totally to God.

When you face up to Jesus Christ, when you accept him, when you truly trust God, you are simply being yourself, your true self. The whole exercise of our religion – the prayers we say, attendance at Mass, our efforts to keep God's laws – is all one lifelong effort to look into Jesus Christ the mirror, to see him looking back at us, and to realise that we are looking at our true selves.

Homily given on 2nd Sunday after Christmas
at St. Aloysius' Glasgow.

River Crossings

The Baptism of Jesus marks a fateful
crossing into new territory.

"Heaven opened"
Luke 3:21

Rivers are important markers, and crossing them can
be significant. It is probable that the English had not
heard of Bannock Burn before June 1314: they have
heard of little else since. It was Caesar's fateful
decision to cross the Rubicon which sparked off the
Massive Civil war that racked the Roman Empire.
For the Israelites the Jordan was (indeed still is) the
river of significance: when they crossed it they
entered the promised land. After wandering in the
desert for forty years they come at last to the river
Jordan on the border of the promised land; their
leader is significantly called Joshua (the Hebrew
form of Jesus, meaning Saviour). As they arrive at the
Jordan the waters part; the army moves across; shortly
afterwards they besiege Jericho whose walls topple
helplessly: at last the promised land is theirs.

In the same spirit John baptises at the Jordan: he
is saying in sign language, "pass through this water
again, God is promising a new life on the other side."
The only snag is that nothing seems to happen! Then
one day Jesus comes for Baptism. This time the
waters do not part, but heaven does. And the invasion
that pours through that opening is not an army, but a
dove: symbol of peace; the promised land is not a
piece of territory, but the Kingdom of Heaven; and
the walls to be toppled are the ones we erect around
ourselves to resist the Good News.

Many Christians think that the object of life is

to sit it out here until we die and then (hopefully) go to heaven. Not so. On that day heaven came into our world: "Heaven opened and the Holy Spirit descended on Him ... like a dove. A voice said 'You are my Son, my favour rests on you.'" Jesus has introduced God's Kingdom here among us: we are challenged to help it grow on earth. Jesus, the real Joshua, has invaded the kingdom of Satan, and is bringing the walls of his city tumbling down. The fact that his symbol is a dove, tells us not to look for armies, force and violence, but truth, sincerity and innocence as the weapons of the Kingdom.

Imagine you are there on that fateful day at the Jordan. Will you, like the first disciples, join Jesus, cross that river and battle for his Kingdom? Brave people joined Robert the Bruce, or Julius Caesar. The challenge is, will you cross the Jordan with Jesus the Anointed One? You may think that because the way of Jesus is all about doves, peace and love, it should be straightforward. Think again: the battle to establish the Kingdom of heaven will lead you to Calvary.

Homily given on feast of the Baptism of our Lord in year "C" at St. Aloysius' Glasgow.

The Lenten Way

Lent can enable us to shed our
self-illusions.

*"His love he set on me, so I will rescue
him"*
Psalm 90

Jean-Paul Sartre, the French philosopher, said "man
is a useless passion to be God." It is a perceptive
insight. So much human conduct is the attempt to
over-reach ourselves; to have total self-possession;
dominate the environment, especially other people;
be liberated from every constraint. If you want to see
sharp examples look at Dictators like Hitler or Stalin:
they wanted to act like gods. In the process all who
got in their way had to be crushed.

All too often the ambitions which are praised
and lauded in human conduct are variants of this
"useless passion to be God". Have you noticed, for
instance, how the essence of that story of Adam and
Eve and their temptation is their choice to throw off
the humiliating lowliness of mere creatures and
become as gods, deciding for themselves what is
good and what is evil? The minute they do this the
pathos of their naked condition is exposed: for the
useless passion to be God only exhibits that skinny
bony featherless biped that was and is but dust.

It is revealing therefore that Jesus, who was
already of divine status, actually chose to oppose that
"useless passion", and insisted on taking on a lowly,
dependent, obedient role. How ever often the
tempter pointed out "Since you are the Son of God",
Jesus reacted by insisting that he would only act in
dependence on God. It was as though his passion
was the useful desire to be a creature!

How can we avoid that repulsive exaltation of self, so pervasive in human attitudes, that mentality of pride? Pride which arrogantly acts as God, blinding the mind and debasing desires. The Church proposes three remedies: prayer, penance, and fasting.

Prayer, because we cannot speak to God except as creature to creator: we have to be our small but true selves when we pray. One reason why a person may find it difficult to pray is because it forces them to stop playing God.

Penance in the sense of admitting our sins, as in confession. The whole point about God is that he is perfect, and ridiculous though it sounds we would too easily presume we share the same condition. Each time we admit a sin, even a small one, we recognise our true state: we come down to earth with a bump.

Fasting. Odd is it not that sin started, crudely speaking, by eating an apple! And odd that Jesus, hungry after forty days, refused to make bread in the wilderness to satisfy hunger. Fasting is not of itself a good thing, but it can be a token way of expressing helplessness and need of God: note how Adam and Eve in taking the apple were trying to show power and independence of God. When we "go without" we school ourselves to accept as gifts, in gratitude, those things we do have and enjoy; we see them as coming from the hand of God and not to be presumed upon.

And the reward is that if we act in reliance on God, he will look after us: "For you has he commanded his angels, to keep you in all your ways."

Homily given on 1st Sunday of Lent in year "C"
at Saints Peter and Paul, Mitcham.

Pilgrims Too

A Christian joins Jesus on his pilgrimage.

"Speaking of his passing which he was to accomplish in Jerusalem"
Luke 9:31

Every Muslim is meant at least once during their lives to make a pilgrimage to Mecca. Nowadays with air travel it is not so difficult, but in former times a life's savings, and a couple of years of journeying could well be the sacrifice entailed.

Going on pilgrimage to a sacred place is a feature of all religions. Chaucer's famous Canterbury Tales are about a pilgrimage; many a Catholic here will have been to Lourdes, or Rome, the Holy Land, or perhaps Walsingham. For something very deep in our religious psyche tells us we are on a journey and must get to a destination. Everyone who has been on a pilgrimage will know the peculiar joy that it generates.

The Jewish religion is all about pilgrimage, and two of its greatest pilgrims were Moses and Elijah. Moses a horizontal pilgrim so to speak, for he led the people out of Egypt, through the desert to the border of the Promised Land. Elijah a vertical pilgrim who went up from the earth to heaven in a fiery chariot.

And why do we find these two talking to Jesus? Because Jesus is *the* pilgrim: he really is travelling, and he really will get to his destination; the two ancient prophets speak of it as "his passing which he was to accomplish in Jerusalem".

Any real pilgrimage must tread each painful path to the destination: it is cheating a bit to just go by plane. So too with Jesus; he did not just rocket off to heaven; he plodded through the earth's suffering and pain; in this way he took them with him.

We too are on our way. Let us be prepared to plod the route through life and keep our eyes fixed in hope on our destination: as we do so we get occasional glimpses of something wonderful coming: it is the transfiguration experience showing that there is glory beyond cross and suffering. Jesus shows us the way; we are walking alongside him.

Homily given on 2nd Sunday of Lent in year "C" at Stonyhurst College, Lancs.

Icons: We Need Them

We need someone to imitate.

"You shall have no gods except me"
Exodus 20:3

A popular way to describe certain key people is as icons. Princess Diana was said to have been an icon, certain film stars or pop idols aspire to the same dizzy heights. An icon, it seems, is a model that others imitate; because they are admired they are imitated.

Obviously there can be good icons and bad icons: a good icon like Mother Teresa will encourage admirers in generosity and selflessness. So icons influence conduct. It is in the light of this that I ask you to consider the Ten Commandments.

These commandments are evidently a moral code, a list of the things we must do and must avoid doing if we are to lead good lives. But at the head of them God declares himself as the Icon: "You shall have no gods except me"; he is the one who alone can be safely admired and worshipped as true guide to good conduct. There are two very simple reasons why this is so:

First, God is good. Admire, imitate, follow the ways of the Lord, and you will be basing your ideals on what is good.

Second, God is real. God is not just some picture of what is nice, he makes the good come true. We can trust God when we act rightly, because he creates and sustains the universe: the good prevails because of him.

Some people will claim that they can lead good lives without coming to church, going to Mass, saying prayers – that is without worshipping God –

because they have an instinctive awareness of what is right and wrong. In a perfect world that might be so; but weak creatures like us are easily led: we need to come under the influence of a good icon. And if we do not expose ourselves to the influence of God, there is every likelihood that we will come under the sway of more dubious icons and be led by them. The worship of God is the very basis of a moral life.

One final caution however. All too easily we mould God into our image and likeness: trying to make him like us, rather than learning from him. We have to be like children who learn. To worship God is to submit ourselves to him, to discover his ways, to be taught what we do not know: and we must try to do this every day. Fortunately God has revealed his truth and goodness in Jesus. In Jesus we have the true Icon, the person we can rightly admire and imitate: be like him and your life will be good.

Homily given on 3rd Sunday of Lent in year "B"
at St. Aloysius' Glasgow.

Still Blind

We should bear in mind that in spiritual matters we are blind, and must be guided.

"Since you say 'we see', your guilt remains"
John 9:41

It seems fatuous to cure a man of blindness if he is in the dark, and yet this is what Jesus has done. For our Lord's interest is not so much to enable us to see the objects around us: everyday things like trees and flowers, sun and stars, people and animals. His desire is to get us to perceive the very things we cannot detect with our sight. We do not see God, we do not see angels, we do not see spirits. They may be all around us, they have great power, perhaps they are directing daily events, but we see nothing. Because we do not see them, it is as though they are not there.

The blind man was blind from birth: he was blind before Jesus cured him; more to the point there were things he could not see after Jesus cured him. He had one advantage, he knew what it was to be blind. When Jesus asked him "Do you believe in the Son of Man?", he knew that his new found sight was of no use: he must get directions, he must be guided, he must be shown the way, just as any blind man needs these aids. "Tell me who he is, so that I may believe in him", he says to Jesus. He accepts the guidance and enters the sphere of light, but still he sees nothing. For though he has been cured of blindness, in the spiritual world he is in pitch darkness; being a perceptive man he recognises there are now realities he can see, but others which are still hidden. In this life we have to believe in all sorts of things by faith; it is foolishness to think something is only there when you can see it.

When we were baptised a great miracle took place: we were given sight, or better perhaps, we were given vision. Our souls can now detect the presence of God, of angels, of mysterious realities working away in our lives and in our world. But we see nothing, for we still dwell in the dark; only our faith gives us clues to these ephemeral things that are all about us. When we die a great change will take place: the light will come on, and we will realise that so many things we only half suspected are really there.

Homily given on 4th Sunday of Lent in year "A" at Stonyhurst College, Lancs.

Condemnation

Jesus both condemns sin, and heals sinners. All at a cost to himself.

"Has no one condemned you?"
John 8:10

She stood humiliated and frightened; hostile men pointing fingers; forced before the most dreadful of judges. She had heard about the Nazarene preacher, his severe strictness, his totally exacting demands. He was the one who had said it was adultery even to look at a person lustfully; constantly in his words in the temple he was preaching about fire, about hell, about judgment. She had heard of it all. And now forced before him, they — the officials, the important people — were asking this bearded Ayatollah, Jesus, to pronounce a fatwa on her. "The law orders death by stoning," they pointed out.

Sure enough he bent down and began to write that dreaded fatwa, that irrevocable sentence. She could not read herself, but one by one the elders, as they read it turned pale, and left in haste. Those accusers, so hot in their righteousness, so smug in their certainty; those men who so smoothly condemned a woman for adultery: always a woman, never a man! Now they were having the tables turned on them. The fierce judge was convicting them and they could not stand their ground.

Yet the Nazarene did this at his peril. All the venom that had been directed at the woman would now be turned in furious anger upon him. If the woman was not to be destroyed someone else would have to be; they must not lose face. It would not be long now before a chillingly similar accusation would ring out "We have a law, and according to our law, he ought to die". Then he would be the lonely reject, deserted and scorned.

There was never a man more ferocious in his condemnation of sin than Jesus: no Ayatollah even comes near him. But there was never anyone who understood the depth of human weakness as Jesus did; so deeply that he was prepared to take the blame and punishment for wrong upon himself to help people who had failed. The woman at last found a person who understood her: fathomed the confused blunder of her ways; plumbed the depths of her frailty.

When later she heard the news that the Nazarene Preacher had died upon a cross, she realised what the fatwa was about.

Homily given on 5th Sunday of Lent in year "C" at Stonyhurst College, Lancs.

Ever the King

On the cross Jesus reigns.

"This is the king of the Jews"
Luke 23:38

He was getting all too used to this. Another rebel leader, from Galilee as so often. There had been Hezekiah, named the Chief Brigand; Judas the Galilean, part of an almost dynasty of rebels against Rome; his sons Jacob and Simon had been crucified. It went on and on. Would these fanatical Jews never accept that all rebellions against Rome got crushed, brutally, effectively, with Crucifixion. And now this one from Nazareth, he had led his gang into Jerusalem on a donkey, for heavens sake! Did he hope to crush the might of Rome with a donkey?

But this time Pilate was puzzled. The Jewish leaders had handed him over: a sharp change from their usual tactic of covertly encouraging rebels, while posing as friends of Rome. And they had some weird complaint about blasphemy: apparently the Nazarene talked about being enthroned beside God. Pilate could not make it out. The man had hardly replied to his questions, although he did not deny claiming to be a king; he seemed to be saying king for ever, and king of all things. Did he think of Rome as just a local authority? Anyway he had to be eliminated: they all had to be; Rome must prevail.

As he hung on the cross the pathos of the whole business showed itself: another rebel on either side of him; many in the crowd laughing, a lot curious, some disgusted, his relatives distraught not knowing what to do, the soldiers just doing their job. Dismas hanging beside him could see it all, and he wondered.

He had heard about the Nazarene who in fact refused to join the rebel movements. And he knew about the miracles, the healing, the hope that this strange man had brought to the dispossessed in Galilee. To Dismas, it seemed that this man had not tried to grab power precisely because he possessed it already. And the message on the street was that he could help anyone who would trust him: it was even claimed that once or twice he had raised people from the dead.

It began to dawn on this brigand that maybe somewhere there was someone who could bring life to people, who could bestow peace, who offered true hope, not just earthly rewards. This man hanging next to him seemed destined to rule a kingdom like that. It was worth a try. "Jesus" he said, "remember me when you come into your kingdom." And the reply came back, "Indeed, I promise you, this day you will be with me in paradise."

Maybe Pilate had not succeeded after all. How do you stop a kingdom that is eternal, that continues after death, that can spread anywhere, that lives in the human heart? Rome would eventually fall, but this man's reign continues.

Homily given at the end of Lent at Stonyhurst College, Lancs.

Change

In his Resurrection Jesus has a new and higher life.

"That he must rise from the dead"
John 20:9

Yeast, as we all know, is used to puff up bread, so that instead of being flat, solid, biscuit-like, it becomes airy, light and full of air pockets. Yeast, is also used in brewing where it transforms the nutrients into alcohol, making a liquid intoxicating. So the point about yeast for religious purposes is that it gives us an example of something that changes things.

The resurrection of Jesus, is not like a re-vival: As though a corpse was somehow brought back to life, somewhat as can be achieved in modern medicine with electric shock or such like. Jesus does not "rise from the dead" as you or I might rise from sleep; rather he transforms death into new life, somewhat as we might think of yeast transforming sugar, barley, malt, hops into alcohol. Our Lord, risen, is a life-giving force, rather like yeast. Let us notice a number of points from this:

— First, as yeast works imperceptibly, so Jesus risen from the dead works on us in hidden ways; nonetheless powerful for all that.

— Second, as yeast transforms and enhances things, bringing them to perfection, so Jesus in his Easter power changes us. Our nature is elevated, we acquire powers we may not be aware of, we become the new creation.

— Third, like yeast which is found everywhere, Jesus pervades the whole created order. People are sometimes puzzled by Catholic claims that the bread and wine of the Eucharist are in reality the body of Christ. But from a Christian point of view, this (to change the metaphor) is just the tip of the iceberg. Christ is transforming the whole of creation; everything will be affected by him; all things are being changed into his new world.

On this great feast of the Christian year, we are therefore celebrating the new creation. In the book of Genesis the First Day is the one where God begins his work of creation. Christians rapidly came to see Sunday as indeed the first day: this though is the day in which God in Christ creates the world anew, with an eternal, indestructible life.

Homily given on Easter Sunday at St. Aloysius' Glasgow.

Voluntary Kingdom

The Christian Way has to be voluntary,
then it can work.

"Everything they owned was held in common"
Acts of the Apostles 4:32

Such is the shortness of human memory, that by and large we have forgotten how, but a few decades back, it was seriously believed that Communism would take over the entire globe. By the end of the second world war a fifth of the planet was Communist; then with the revolution of Mao Tse Tung it became a third. Vicious wars were fought in Korea, Vietnam, trying to arrest the inexorable spread of the Communist ideology. But then suddenly it all collapsed and seems to have disappeared without trace.

Their original idea was that money was just a trick for exploiting people: those who had it gained power over those who didn't: not entirely a mistaken notion by any means. St Paul himself said "The love of money is the root of all evil." But communism as it developed tried to force the abolition of property; to do this it had to exercise power over everyone; and thus it resorted to the very tyranny and bullying which it was trying to abolish.

A very different kind of Communism can be found in Christianity; its motivation is mutual trust and goodwill, leading people to share what they have with others. The Acts of the Apostles introduces the first Christians as having no property of their own, and attempts have been made to continue this ideal down the centuries. Religious congregations, like the Franciscans, all take a vow of poverty: the monks or sisters have no property of their own, but everything is held in common. The very familiar practice of charity – giving to those in need, is an attempt to share. And the ideal Christian family is one where everyone shares whatever there is.

Homily given on 2nd Sunday of Easter in year "B" at St. Aloysius' Glasgow.

The Scriptures

The Scriptures tell us about Christ, but not in an obvious way.

"Ordained that the Christ would suffer, and so enter into his glory"
Luke 24:26

To claim that the Old Testament tells us about the resurrection of Jesus is odd, because by and large Jewish people in Old Testament times did not believe in a life after death. This explains the great emphasis on having children, and the fear of barrenness: in one's offspring, name, status and hopes were continued. Abraham, you will notice, is not promised eternal life, but "I will make your descendants like the dust on the ground, too many to be counted."

The claim that the Messiah would suffer and die is an odd one too, since God should surely protect his servant from evil men. Muslims cannot stomach the notion that Christ was crucified: they resort to saying someone else, perhaps Simon of Cyrene, was crucified by mistake. Take the case of Muhammad himself: they say, he was persecuted and driven out of Mecca on 16 July 622 (the first day of the Muslim era). But after much suffering he eventually returned in triumph to Mecca in 629. Surely, they assert, God would give victory to his prophet Jesus in Jerusalem as he did to his prophet Muhammad in Mecca. Indeed it has to be admitted that the great figures of the Scriptures: Moses, Abraham, David, are victorious heroes: no death or crucifixion for them. At the time of Jesus' crucifixion his enemies thought his execution would prove he was an imposter: "If you are the Christ, come down from the cross."

In order to explain our Christian faith, we will have to resort to arguing that Jesus fulfilled the Scriptures in a mysterious and paradoxical way. There must be some deeper meaning in Scripture that is not noticed at first sight. And if this is so, surely there is some undetected significance in suffering and death.

Has Christianity ever swallowed this troublesome truth? In a simplistic view the pursuit of health, wealth and happiness is everything: where it is achieved, God's blessing is discerned; whilst poverty, sickness, etc. are seen as God's curse and disfavour. Even the disciples had this attitude: for them the death of Jesus induced disaster and despair.

The peculiar role of suffering, failure, even death as the path to God, as the road to resurrection triumph is perhaps the great Christian insight. What a mystery is here! How completely different from popular expectations and thoughts! So strange was the way of Christ, not even his closest followers understood him.

And how profound must the Scriptures be, if all the time they were really telling us about Messiah crucified and risen, while no one saw it.

Homily given on 3rd Sunday of Easter in year "A" at St. Aloysius' Glasgow.

Direct Guidance

In some ways we are led directly by God.

"The sheep follow because they know his voice"
John 10:4

St John's profound Gospel is very keen to insist that the Christian is led directly by God, needing no other guide. We all know how a lamb can recognise the bleat of its mother; and along the same lines Jesus says that his followers "know his voice" and will not follow a stranger. It is a very strong doctrine, that we are taught directly by God, and it is found in some of the toughest Christian bodies. For example, the Quakers who refuse to accept any church, and do not have sacraments such as baptism or Holy Communion, believe there is an interior light that will guide anyone who is willing to seek: and it is remarkable that the Society of Friends, as they are called, has produced powerful social reformers and people of highest principles. One of their great convictions is that "there is a bit of God in all of us".

And of course the reason why a lamb knows its mother's bleat, is that it has the ewe's genetic code: the lamb has something of its mother imprinted on its memory. In the same way, through the Holy Spirit within us, there is a presence of God in our very souls, so we can recognise the heavenly call and know its comforting sound.

This is all true; but unfortunately there is a problem. I once lived at a college in the country set against a park full of sheep. One evening as dusk was falling, a small lamb began to bleat for its mother. After a couple of seconds the unmistakable reply call

117

came back and the lamb ran towards it, still calling repeatedly as they do; again and again the response came back, promptly and clearly: so re-assuring! But when the lamb got right up to the college walls, there was no mother sheep there: the little animal had in fact been picking up the echo of its own bleat, bouncing off the walls. How do we know that we are listening to the voice of God, and not just an echo of our own sound? Or worse, how does the little girl know that Grandma with her very big eyes, remarkable big ears, and excellently preserved teeth is really grandma?

Thus in his First Letter St John tells us to test the inner light, because not every spirit comes from God. We can only recognise the voice of God within us if we:

a. Have sound doctrine
b. Take spiritual duties like prayer and sacraments seriously.
c. Are willing to honestly admit our sins and failings.

But given these things a Christian genuinely can hear the voice. Catholics are all too apt to assume that we are meant to be sheepish in the bad sense, simply doing what we are told, and expecting others to make decisions, to know the ways of God, to supply our deficiencies. This is a mistake. Without in any way claiming to be superior, or rejecting guidance from others, we must seriously consider that the Lord does speak to us, guide us, lead us; individually, in our souls. We must ever seek the light within, make sure our consciences remain attuned to God's ways, and hope for guidance.

Homily given on 4th Sunday of Easter in year "A"
at Stonyhurst College, Lancs.

Conscience

Conscience is very powerful, and
dangerous when perverted.

*"Only by this can we be certain that we
are children of the truth, and be able to
quieten our conscience in his presence"*
First Letter of St John 3:19

The great psychologist Carl Gustav Jung, lived in
Switzerland when the Nazis were coming to power
in Germany; from his site safely over the border he
was able to analyse their conduct and motives, and
diagnose what was possessing their minds.

After a time he noticed an astonishing thing:
whilst their hatred focused on the Jews, picking out
their characteristics, real or imagined, with violent
repulsion, the Nazi movement showed the same
characteristics itself. Jews were said to be a race apart:
the Nazis claimed to lead a master race; Jews were
thought to dominate the world: this is what the
Nazis intended to do; Jews were reviled as the
divinely chosen people: the Nazis were obsessed
with dreams of their destiny; Jews went back as a
people into very early times: the Nazis claimed to
discover ancient Teuton tribes from which their
culture came; Jews kept their people together
through marriage: the Nazis were to forbid marriage
to non-Aryans.

And so Jung concluded that all that insane hatred
against Jews was really merely a projection of a hatred
they really felt for themselves. And indeed one
notices that Hitler's dreadful campaign to exterminate
the Jews coincided with his own death-wish whereby

he fought the war in a manner that guaranteed his own and Germany's final devastation.

All of this gives us an insight into the most powerful force within us: I mean conscience. It has been aptly said that conscience is the voice of God. No one can get away from endlessly judging each event in terms of right and wrong; we all feel a desperate need to condemn evil, for that demanding voice constantly requires us to take a stand on any conduct. So insistent is our conscience that if we find it too painful to admit wrongs in ourselves, we perversely search out or even pretend to find wickedness in others instead. It is well known that convicted criminals are very indignant about child molesters, because in this way they can vent the demand of their conscience for justice onto other offenders. We can blind ourselves to conscience only by perverting it: what we cannot acknowledge in ourselves we will promptly claim to perceive and condemn in others; and in our sad desperation we end up not knowing what is right or wrong, however indignant we feel.

Saint John in his letter tells us that only by accepting our sinfulness and throwing ourselves upon God can we have peace. No person is more dangerous than the moraliser; without a profound knowledge of our sinfulness and the perversity it sows in our outlook we cannot begin; but with a great sense of the grace, mercy and healing of God, we are able to face ourselves, and then orientate on others in an attitude of love rather than judgement.

Indeed, armed with the assurance of God's forgiving love shown in Jesus, we will learn to love and accept ourselves, happily admitting our defects. And when we humbly love ourselves, sinners though we be, we can love others too, sinners though they be. If only the Nazis had been able to do this, they would never have destroyed six million Jews; they would not have destroyed themselves either.

Homily given on 5th Sunday of Easter in year "B" at St. Aloysius' Glasgow.

Successful Love

The right kind of love works, it is successful.

"Remain in my love"
John 15:9

To love is to share the goodness that is within us. But we can only give what we have got. People do love, but their sharing gets contaminated by their envy, pride, jealousy, selfishness. This is why there is so much disappointment in human relationships: between married partners, between parents and children, even between nation states. We do love, but we struggle to love successfully.

Love is like a kind of currency. Just as a currency can become debased if notes are forged, or stolen ones are circulated, or the government merely prints millions of new ones; so too our loves get mixed in with all kinds of dubious passions, and real love gets poisoned: from then on it ceases to work.

Jesus' love is pure: it is selfless and nothing but love. He proves his genuineness by laying down his life for us: that is real love. If only we had that love, we could share a real goodness. And the good news of the Gospel is that if we keep his commandments, we will share his love. It will make our love for our family, for our friends, and for strangers too, real, successful, truly helpful. This clearly is a currency worth having.

So many people today are genuinely trying to care, to make lasting relationships, to bring help to others. They are puzzled to find that their efforts so often end in failure: they do love, but they do not love successfully! For they suppose they can achieve success through sentiment, through just wanting to do good. But our Lord tells us that we must follow his commandments to remain in his love, the love that works. It is a matter of having the right method, not just a hopeful attitude. We cannot compromise on this.

Notice how our Lord tells us that he wants us to go out and bear fruit. The proof of genuine love is that it has good results; for love is a sharing of goodness that enables the other to blossom as a result. Jesus actually had the power to give his own life so that we can grow and flourish: if we keep his commandments he will give us the same power.

Homily given on 6th Sunday of Easter in year "B" at St. Aloysius' Glasgow.

Save the World!

The job of the Christian is to make this world better.

"I am not asking you to remove them from the world"
John 11:15

It is often claimed that Christianity is a form of escapism, that it promises "pie in the sky when you die", that it tells people simply to endure this life, and hope for a better existence in some heavenly sphere after death.

And this on the face of it is what Jesus appears to say: "they do not belong to the world, any more than I belong to the world". But then he qualifies this by saying "I am not asking you to remove them from the world", and points out "I have sent them in to the world".

Far from forsaking the world, Jesus reclaimed it for God. At the end of his life he did not die and "go to heaven" (whatever that means) he rose from the dead. He transformed his own body, but stayed in it: a body that is part of God's creation, part of the world which he would not abandon. And the book of Revelation speaks, not about Christians leaving this world and "going to heaven", but of this world becoming heaven: "Then I saw a new heaven and a new earth, ... I saw the holy city, the new Jerusalem, coming down out of heaven from God. And the one sitting on the throne said, "Look, I am making the whole of creation new."

It might have been a lot easier for those disciples if Jesus had said in effect "Hang on for a few more years, then you can leave all this mess, and go to heaven"; but he did not, he said "I have sent them into the world". In the same way it may seem easier for us, to just suffer this existence, and wait for a better. But that will not do: we are commissioned to transform the world into a better place; and those who want to know what this will cost should take a careful look at a crucifix.

But in order to accomplish our task we are told we must not "belong to the world". We are to live on this alien planet and change it, so that it becomes heaven: no mean task.

The disciples were full of foreboding at the prospect ahead of them: how were they to go forward in this task, and with Jesus gone? How will we do so?

– First, by living a life of faith. I mean one where we see that Jesus sends power to us from the throne of God; power especially through the gift of the Holy Spirit.

– Second, by getting our perspective right. Jesus has won the victory over Satan already: we are engaged in what military minds call a "mopping up operation". Let us stop demoralising ourselves with tales of the triumph of evil: the victory is already ours.

– Third, by living a spiritual life: one where we derive our strength from prayer, sacraments, Christian company; where we, so to speak, 'plug in' to heavenly resources. It will give you an idea of what I mean if I close with this illustration of its opposite:

Radio 4 had an item last week on drug use and the rapid spread of crack cocaine for what is called recreational purposes. One or two who spoke claimed that it enabled them to function better;

made them more dynamic and energetic. You may well wonder about that. But our claim as Christians, is that there are heavenly resources available to us, that enable us to do the work of our Lord in this difficult world: it is the knack of using those resources that constitutes the spiritual life of the Christian.

Homily given on 7th Sunday of Easter in year "B"
at Stonyhurst College, Lancs.

Share the Victory!

Jesus sends his disciples to work in this world, and to reclaim it for God.

"Why are you men of Galilee standing here looking up into the sky?"
Acts of the Apostles 1:11

Ever fearful of military dictatorships, the Roman Republic forbad any legion to reside in the city of Rome. Thus the world's greatest military power, was totally without troops in its own capital city. The only time a Roman Army might enter the imperial city was after a great victory, when the Senate would allow them a Triumph: a parade through the city hauling all the spoils and booty from their conquering campaign. The magnificent sight of the bronzed legions, horse-drawn chariots, plumed helmets, shining armour, might well inspire the young Roman citizen to seek to join the army and get in on the next campaign; but the sight only lasted a day, before the army disappeared from the streets.

For a short moment the disciples saw Jesus triumphant, then he vanished from their sight. In a whirlwind of triumph Jesus, having subdued and conquered the forces of evil, passed by the disciples and ascended into glory. For ever after Christians have hymned his conquest in the "Gloria": this may start with the angelic proclamation of Christmas night "Glory to God in the highest", but quickly moves to the praise of Christ triumphant: "You are seated at the right hand of the Father, you alone are the holy one, you alone Lord, Most High Jesus Christ to the glory of God the Father."

Jesus has fought his battle; won his victory! What

127

about us? Will we just admire the great triumph, and then go home? Like the disciples gaze skywards, helplessly? The battle against evil must be fought again in each generation: Jesus has shown it can be won; Jesus gives us power to win it. But we must follow his inspiration and join the force.

"Don't just stand there", was the message of the angels to the heavenward gazing disciples. "Go into the whole world, and proclaim the Good News to everybody" Jesus had told them. That is what we must do: for out there is a vast mass of people helplessly ensnared by negative forces – we, the followers of Jesus, can help them.

Homily given on the feast of the Ascension of our Lord in year "C" at Stonyhurst College, Lancs.

Divine Influence

The Holy Spirit brings a healing power,
not force or aggression.

"They were all filled with the Holy Spirit"
Acts of the Apostles 2:4

The action of Pakistan in exploding atom bombs this week, in reply to the same action by India a month or so earlier; the way both peoples danced in the street on hearing the news – it all reminds us of the insatiable desire of humans to be powerful. Not that we in the West can take a holier than thou attitude: the very same desire to have our own bomb inspired the United States, Russia, Britain, France to build these terrible weapons. A German psychologist claimed that much human conduct can be explained as the Will to Power: a desire to conquer everywhere as we have seen in Hitler, Stalin, Pol Pot and so many others this century.

Such an irony then, that this so forceful pursuit always seems to end in failure. All these mighty conquerors collapse under the weight of their own aggression and disappear into the graves of history. Like atom bombs they can wreak great destruction, but achieve no construction.

One would hardly think of the small group assembled in the room in Jerusalem as setting out to conquer the world: but that is what they were about to do. Within minutes of their strange experience it became apparent that they had access to all hearts: Parthians, Egyptians, Libyans, Romans; there were no barriers to stop them. Somehow the Holy Spirit would lead them to world conquest not by universal destruction, but by the balm and healing of a gentle presence, gifts of understanding and peace, thoughts of harmony and acceptance.

For be in no doubt the one conquest of the world that has ever lasted, perhaps because no one was ever conquered or crushed by its coming, was begun on that Pentecost day. From that point a huge universal movement enrolled into its citizenship every kind and condition of people. It did not rely on power, it did not spread by force; it was the work of that gentle divine influence – the Holy Spirit.

When today, so much emphasis is placed on nuclear weapons and the pride that nations derive from them, it is incumbent on us Christians to bring a very different attitude to humanity: one which knows no barriers, no antagonism; one which forms us all into the great family of God.

Yet how do we get the Holy Spirit to come to us? Very simple: it is when we are gathered together in prayer that the Spirit comes down.

Homily given on Pentecost Sunday at St. Aloysius' Glasgow.

Harmony

The Holy Trinity can be thought of as like a family that is perfectly one.

"God loved the world so much that he gave his only Son"
John 3:16

Unhappily, mention of the Holy Trinity produces an instant sense of boredom and vagueness. Somehow we think it is all abstract, a kind of mathematical conundrum proving that three is one; we are told to think of triangles, and other abstruse concepts: the very examples used to produce understanding are themselves obscure.

I want to suggest to you that if we think of God as a kind of family, we will be on the right lines. Imagine a perfect family, where there is giving and taking, mutual understanding and sharing; respect for individuality, but harmony among all. Is not God like this? God is not to be thought of as some lonely old man in the sky, creating the world to relieve the boredom and looking down on his creatures curiously, in the way that we look at animals in a zoo! No, from all eternity, there has been in the very heart of God, so to speak, a great activity of loving, giving and taking, sharing and caring.

We know that in human life nothing so destroys a person as isolation, especially when someone isolates themselves, perhaps because they are bitter, drowned by sorrow, eaten up with jealousy, raging with anger; and nothing so makes a person grow as relating to other people, as when we know friendship, have trust, learn to accept and forgive. We are human through other people. So too with God, it is that rich love, sharing, and life in the heart of the Trinity that makes God what he is.

And it is in this divine life that we see lived out the solutions to a puzzle that taxes the modern mind. For our age very much wishes to believe in equality, and it very much wishes to believe in individuality. Now in God we find both of these: Father, Son and Holy Ghost are utterly equal: each has what the others have: there is no greater versus lesser; and yet The Father is not the Son, nor the Son the Spirit, nor the Spirit the Father: each person has a true identity. This perfect oneness going hand in hand with complete individuality only occurs, of course, where there is perfect love.

Love and happiness of their nature tend to spread; so it is not surprising that this God who is so full of life, should choose to share what he has with us creatures. The line we heard in today's Gospel, supposed to be the best known line in the bible, says it so poignantly "God loved the world so much, that he gave his only Son".

But we should not simply think that God entered our world on a sort of visit of pity, as one might go to a refugee camp and later leave again. Incredible though it sounds, through Jesus God the Father is extending an invitation to come and join the family. We are being invited, for all our unworthiness, to come into that heart of God where all life is lived.

Homily given on Trinity Sunday in year "A"
at Stonyhurst College, Lancs.

Souls

We should not too readily talk of people who have died as in heaven: they may need our prayers.

"That they may be released from their sins"
2 Maccabees 12:45

An odd religious group can be found in the world today: they are called Christians. One of the peculiar notions they have is that there is a place called Heaven where they go when they die. I used to believe all this myself, until one day, shortly after the first landing on the moon in the 1970s, I was asked by a seven-year-old child in a primary school, why the spacemen had not come across heaven during their journey. Of course I explained that heaven is just the far side of the moon: had they gone a bit further they would doubtless have seen it. But now as we go deeper and deeper into space, it is beginning to look as though the young lad had a point! Could it be that heaven is not so much a place? Maybe heaven is a future that is going to happen.

Jesus himself spoke of the Kingdom of Heaven drawing near, and warned us to be ready for it: surely we are waiting for heaven. And even though it sounds very simple, is it not true that a dead person is in their grave? It is obvious they are not in heaven. The Christian belief is that when we die, we must wait, we cannot just "go to heaven"; indeed prayers of the kind "may they rest in peace", imply that the dead are waiting.

Although we have little knowledge of how it is to have died, yet not be in a heavenly state, we may suppose that in some dim way it would be a state of anxiety. Rather as a person being sedated for a major operation, has a sense of foreboding, feeling helpless and passive, but knowing that a great deal depends on the outcome of the next few hours; so at death we know we are passing through a crisis, but are not sure of the outcome. The departed soul may even have a sense of fear, from an awareness of sins they have carried to the grave, and the fact that they are awaiting judgement.

Hence the reaction of the Maccabee leaders towards their fallen comrades: they prayed for them "that they might be released from their sin". We must all take on board the true reality of death: even Jesus remained dead for three days and then rose from the dead. Our deceased friends and relatives have not yet risen from the dead: they are still lying in their graves. We must pray that they may be comforted and reassured there, until the great event when Jesus Christ finally establishes the Kingdom of Heaven here; raises them from their graves; and (as we may hope) judges them worthy to dwell in his kingdom.

Homily for All Souls day given at St. Aloysius' Glasgow.

How We See Things

There is life, but also higher kinds of life. It is a higher kind that is offered to us.

"Anyone who eats this bread will live forever"
John 6:51

The planet Mars, often called the red planet, appears to be all desert: some kind of red sand and stones covering its entire surface. It has, it would seem, no form of life, and scientists assure us that without water, life such as we find on earth cannot be sustained.

It was therefore a wonderful discovery of the last few weeks, that just beneath this layer of rock and sand great lochs of water lie untouched. In principle it will be possible now for explorers to go from earth and use the water to sustain themselves whilst on Mars.

If we could enter the mind of some of those scientists at NASA, and see how they perceived Mars when they supposed it was simply dry desert, and then observe how they now perceive it, having discovered that it holds water, I am sure we would find they now see Mars differently. They see it as lively, welcoming, hopeful, life-giving; whereas before they must have thought of it as a kind of graveyard.

Now I put it to you that it is the same for us with the Blessed Eucharist. If we think of the host and chalice as merely bread and wine; if we suppose we are but eating ordinary things when we go to Holy Communion, we will be like people who think of Mars as a desert. On the other hand once we recognise that beneath that appearance of bread and wine lies the true reality: Jesus Christ, risen from the dead, whole and entire, seated at the right hand of the Father even as he comes to us; Jesus Christ conqueror of death, forgiving sin, healing sickness; Jesus Christ, for whom and through whom this whole universe was created, the Alpha and Omega, the beginning of all things and their end. If we recognise all this, then we will find life here; life in fullness.

We should think that we are on a journey more challenging than that of explorers landing on Mars, for we are journeying to eternal life. We will need powerful sustenance to keep going, and this only Jesus himself can give us. Let us be careful to recognise Him in the Eucharist for what he really is: to have reverence, esteem, faith: to know that it is He whom we must have if we are to make the journey successfully.

Homily given on the Feast of the Body and Blood of Christ in year "A" at Stonyhurst College, Lancs.

Misguided

Great patience may be needed in an
authentic Christian life.

"How happy are the poor in spirit"
Matthew 5:3

Because of fears of the plague the planned opening
of Parliament in 1605 was postponed from February
to 3rd October; and in the event anxiety that the
dreaded disease still lingered, caused it to be
postponed yet again, so that the new date chosen
that year was Tuesday 5th November.

All this time a group of very sincere, very courageous, but fatally misguided Catholic young men
were developing a most extraordinary plot. Mad-
dened by the continuing persecution of Catholics
they planned to blow up the Houses of Parliament.
The government got to know about it, and carefully
timing their coup pretended to discover the plot at
the very last moment. Inspecting the vaults of the
house around midnight on 4th November, they
noticed someone lurking in the shadows and arrested
him. He gave his name as Guido Johnson; in fact it
was Guy Fawkes.

You know it is not easy to be a saint. Robert
Catesby, Guy Fawkes and the thirteen plotters gave
their lives for what they believed in, suffered horrible
tortures and ignominious deaths, but what they did
was wrong. It gave a cunning government a
wonderful excuse to persecute all Catholics, and
generate a propaganda war that has lasted almost to
this day. Innocent men like Fr Henry Garnet were
executed, and honest women like Anne Vaux

imprisoned in the hysterical hue and cry which resulted.

The plotters were not saints because in their desperation under persecution they ceased to trust in God and began to hope in sheer force. From our comfortable position it is easy for us to blame them, but we would do better to remember that each of us can easily be deluded. Do we trust God when things are difficult? Do we rely on his help? Do we suppose that any remedy for our problems must take the form of action, perhaps selfish or ruthless action of our own? We would do well to follow the advice of that wonderful Psalm – Psalm 36:

> *If you trust in the Lord and do good,*
> *then you will live in the land and be secure.*
>
> *Commit your life to the Lord,*
> *trust in him and he will act.*
>
> *Be still before the Lord and wait in patience;*
> *do not fret at the man who prospers.*
>
> *Calm your anger and forget your rage,*
> *do not fret, it only leads to evil.*
>
> *The salvation of the just comes from the Lord,*
> *their stronghold in time of distress.*
>
> *The Lord helps them and delivers them*
> *and saves them: for their refuge is in him.*

Homily given on the Feast of All Saints
at Stonyhurst College, Lancs.

No Dream

This homily was given in the context of the feast of Candlemas.

"A light to enlighten the pagans"
Luke 2:32

G.K. Chesterton has a poem about a baby in the womb who dreams of some marvellous place where green hair grows on hills, a huge warming fire lurks in the sky, and somehow all the water has been painted a deep blue: the child of course wants to be born into this fantastic fairyland, and says:

> *I think that if they gave me leave*
> *within that world to stand*
> *I would be good through all the day*
> *I spent in fairyland.*

If only we could see the world as a child does, as one terrific miracle: for the most astonishing truth of all truths are the things around us: trees, mountains, planes, planets, people: anything is amazing by the very fact that it is something: it is not nothing.

And this was the profound insight of that saint whose feast occurred during the week: St Thomas Aquinas. Aquinas was a Dominican monk; you would expect him to have his head in the clouds writing his famous five arguments for the existence of God; all that spiritual stuff. But Aquinas was only interested in things; the things all around us: what puzzled him, fascinated him, interested him was the fact that anything is: that is the great truth, and it contains the clue to all other truths. If something exists, then there is existence; and ultimately there

139

must be self existence: God: who is there without depending on anything else.

Aquinas attained in adulthood, that great insight we all had as children: the world around us is fabulous; you would never believe it if you had not seen it; it is too wonderful to be true, except that it is there and patently true. Once you see that the ordinary is fantastic, you have no problem with preposterous ideas like God, who always is; you begin to see that the world is as a self portrait, painted by its creator.

Simeon was one of a number of people who came across an ordinary little child in the temple that day, with his simple rural mother and father; Simeon saw that ordinary child and knew he had found an extra-ordinary child; he looked at a creature and he saw his creator; he decided his time had come because he had found eternity; like Thomas Aquinas he rested, because now he gazed on the great truth: in that tiny child he saw God.

Homily on St. Thomas Aquinas given on the Feast of Candlemas at Stonyhurst College, Lancs.

Destiny

In a mysterious way our bodies have a heavenly destination.

"May we see heaven as our final goal"
From the Opening Prayer of the Mass of the Assumption of our Lady.

Gravestones, as we have been reminded this week, can have all sorts of inscriptions on them. Some try to be witty like the one which said:

> *Here lies Fred, who was alive, but is dead.*
> *Had it been his Father, I had much rather,*
> *Had it been his Mother, still better than another,*
> *Had it been his Sister, no one would have missed her.*
> *But since 'tis only Fred, that was alive and is dead,*
> *there's nothing more to be said.*

Others engrave on the memorial at the final resting place a message which is serious but inspiring. Thus on the tomb of General William Booth, founder of the Salvation Army, we read:

> *William Booth. Born 1829. Reborn 1844 (a reference to his conversion). Promoted to Glory 1912.*

Evidently in saying that this man has been "Promoted to Glory", we are being advised to raise our sights beyond a dead corpse under that stone, to that elevated heavenly state where the blessed dwell in the celestial light.

The resurrection of Jesus was Promotion to Glory, so complete in his case that nothing is left behind: there is no body: he is entirely in heaven. And we believe that Mary mother of Jesus was herself made perfect to that point where her body did not remain, and no tomb enclosed her: she has gone entirely to glory.

Why, from all fallen mankind, has this woman been so utterly blest by God? And what do we see in her life to convince us of her outstanding holiness?

It must be in the way she gave her heart at the Lord's invitation, unswervingly devoting her whole future as a young girl to God's plan, without musing on the unnerving demands this was to make on her. So total was her commitment that it was she who at Cana urged her Son into that life of preaching that led to the cross, a cross where she was present and undeviating as much as he. She was the one who rallied the first followers, encouraging them to be wholehearted disciples of the risen Christ, as in prayer they sought strength awaiting the Holy Spirit.

Yet in her very ordinariness as a Jewish wife from Nazareth we see the astonishing truth that Christ can grow in any human heart: so many whose lives are plain are yet moulded into saints. These men and women, our great cloud of witnesses, all show us that it is possible to say "yes" to God, even through an entire life: with Mary these blessed ones ever encourage us to rally to the standard of Christ.

The time will come when you will die, be placed in the earth; your relatives will consider what appropriate line can be engraved on your monument. Would they be able, honestly, fairly, accurately to carve in stone next to your name "promoted to glory"?

Homily Given on the Feast of the Assumption of our Lady at Sacred Heart, Wimbledon.

Join It!

Truth has a power that persists through time.

"I came into the world for this: to bear witness to the truth"
John 18:37

Josef Stalin, perhaps a greater tyrant than Adolf Hitler, on hearing Winston Churchill's objection that the Pope would not like to see Poland overrun by the Communist armies, responded sarcastically: "And how many Divisions, Mr Churchill, has the Pope?" Had he lived long enough Stalin would have seen in that very country a force greater than his military machine, one which actually overthrew it.

People do tend to think of Jesus Christ, of Christianity, as nice but impotent. If they are vicious people, like Stalin, they think Christianity can be brushed aside like a fly; rather better disposed persons, suppose Christianity to be but a spent force from previous ages: what a pity they do not look at the twentieth century.

That strange last book of the new Testament, the Apocalypse or Revelation, is constantly talking about power issuing from fabled creatures, good or bad: the dragon spews out a great river of water to try and drown the woman; the beast sends out from its mouth a foul spirit, like a frog; but in contrast to these, Jesus Christ, the faithful witness appears, and from his mouth comes a sharp sword. This sword, is the truth which Jesus speaks from God, a truth that is "alive and active, cutting more keenly than any two edged sword, sifting the purposes and thoughts of the heart". As Pilate was to discover "There is nothing in creation that can hide from him; everything lies naked and exposed to the eyes of the One with whom we have to reckon."

Jesus is as powerful today as ever: his truth cuts through the shams of the twentieth century as surely as it cut through the arguments of Pilate. The power of truth works silently, works on the heart; for this reason many do not notice it. But Christ and his Word live on today, whilst the power of Stalin and his ideology has evaporated.

It used to be said when Communism seemed to be growing inexorably, seeming to be taking over the globe: "If you can't beat it, join it." The slogan would be better applied to Christianity.

Homily given on the Feast of Christ the King in year "B" at St. Aloysius' Glasgow.

Ugly Love

In the story, Pip is forced to accept that he has been helped by a repulsive looking criminal, Magwitch. Love has proved stronger than appearances.

Hosea 11:1,4

THE SACRED HEART OF JESUS

Perhaps the greatest story of Charles Dickens is found in *Great Expectations*, where the young man Pip prospers wonderfully, blithely unaware that a convict he encountered as a boy is putting money into his bank account. Eventually at the risk of his life the convict returns from Australia to meet Pip, whose initial reaction to this uncouth thug is revulsion and disgust. But it slowly comes home that the old criminal has loved him, and this moves his heart.

Last Friday we had the feast of the Sacred Heart of Jesus. Through his Heart, Jesus discloses to us that he has cherished us even to the point of death: "One of the soldiers pierced his side with a lance, and there flowed out blood and water." This love is nothing less that the love of God for us. In a sense Jesus seems to have done little for people: not much of a politician – no increase in prosperity, national greatness – in many ways people were disappointed with him. All he gave was love, and that can seem a rather useless gift.

And we should notice that the love of Jesus for us is the fulfilment of God's care for his people proclaimed in the Old Testament where it is declared again and again. Thus Hosea the prophet has this message:

Israel in his boyhood what love I bore him!
and I called my son out of Egypt.
It was I, none other, guided those first steps of
*   theirs,*
and took them in my arms,
*   and healed, all unobserved their injuries.*

So why do we not recognise the love of our Lord for us? Perhaps for the same reasons as Pip in Great Expectations. On the one hand taking God's blessings so much for granted, we barely notice them, on the other when we do meet love it may be as a rough uncouth affair, like the criminal Magwitch, half his teeth missing, suddenly knocking on Pip's door. Think of it, the crowd standing around at the crucifixion would have seen a wretched and repulsive criminal, flies buzzing about his head, they would not easily have realised that in his very death Jesus was giving all he had for them.

So let us try to meet the request of Jesus in those revelations of his Sacred Heart to St Margaret Mary in the seventeenth century, wherein he asked us to strive to comprehend his love. Then we will find how warm it is, how human, how caring; and then we will obtain access to him. As the fourteenth-century mystical treatise "The Cloud of Unknowing" puts it so profoundly "By love he can be caught and held, by thinking never."

Homily given after the feast of the Sacred Heart of Jesus
in St. Aloysius' Glasgow.

Two Opposites

This homily was given in the church in Mitcham, which is dedicated to Saints Peter and Paul.

"Once they saw that the gospel for the uncircumcised had been entrusted to me, just as to Peter the gospel to the circumcised."
Galatians 2:7

SAINTS PETER AND PAUL

The most famous storybook pair of detectives are Sherlock Holmes and Dr Watson. The two make such a contrast that each sets off the special features of the other; Holmes so sharp and dynamic, Watson cautious but solid. Holmes finds everything elementary, Watson is always puzzled. Holmes has fits of excitement followed by bouts of depression; Watson the dependable doctor, ever on an even keel.

St Peter and St Paul are a pair like that: two very diverse personalities: the very special characteristics of the one, causes us to notice the opposite features in the other.

Paul so learned, so sure of himself, a brilliant preacher, an able teacher, a competent organiser. Here was a man who travelled the world, held the precious Roman Citizenship, studied under renowned Rabbi Gamaliel, preached in the forum at Athens, argued in court in Hebrew, Greek or Latin. A formidable, striking and distinguished man. Yet Paul had never seen Jesus: his bold faith was exactly that, believing in what he had not observed.

Peter a simple fisherman, probably never left Galilee until Jesus came for him. A shy, humble, but very genuine person. He would have loved to stay in

Galilee in those country places where the first disciples had wandered with Jesus; he found it terribly difficult to adapt to the new world opening up as the Christian way rapidly expanded into the Roman Empire; and although he was by Jesus' own appointment the leader of the Christian disciples, he seems to have been rather overwhelmed by the task.

If we thought of Paul alone, we might be put off by such a bold, dominating character; if we thought of Peter by himself we might think poorly of him as a rude unlettered peasant. But when we put the two side by side, what a marvel we see: this is what the power of Christ has done; this is how people so very different can do such wonderful things; this is how God makes use of a person as they are and turns their characteristics to great good.

And so it is with us. In our parish of St Peter and Paul we are many distinct personalities. Each of us is important, and one's special characteristics show up the unique qualities of another. We can reflect that Jesus has a special job for me personally to do for him; then we must fully accept that each other soul has their special call. And let us bear in mind that what really made both Peter and Paul so momentous in early Christian Life was their close friendship with Jesus: the Jesus who strode through Galilee and the Jesus risen from the dead. We too can have that, we too can share in the great Apostles' work, we too can bring the Good News to Mitcham.

On this feast of these two great missionaries therefore, we ask the Lord that we may share in their Spirit to spread his Kingdom: in the bold confidence of Paul to stand up for our faith in public, in the simple sincere discipleship of Peter to preserve our Christian values at home.

Homily given on the feast of Saints Peter and Paul at the Church of Saints Peter and Paul, Mitcham.

Life Given by Death

Jesus does not merely share; he gives his very self.

"You are proclaiming his death"
1 Corinthians 11:26

The Corinthians were an enthusiastic bunch, but unruly and almost out of control. Paul complained that when they assembled as a Christian Community, they generated scenes of chaos, many shouting out together, demanding attention with the claim that they were uttering messages from the Holy Spirit. But what really niggled Paul, was that various families were turning up with their own provisions: rich ones with fine wines, hampers from Harrods, waiter service; whilst the poor ones, often slaves, could only come penniless, hungrily watching their fellow Christians living it up.

Paul's criticism of this is sharp. He does not merely say that people who care should share, or point to some common decency that you would look for in any group. As always he goes for the dramatic. He tells the story of the man who at a meal did not just share his food, but shared himself; he tells the story of the man who when he was about to die, gave his life to his companions; he tells the story of the man whose death sustains them.

Maybe it came as a shock, or at least a surprise to those selfish Corinthians, to be reminded of the Jesus who having once fed five thousand with bread and fish, ended up nurturing his friends by giving them his own life: "This is my body which is for you." Perhaps they were encouraged to hear that Jesus wanted to forge a permanent friendship by his death: "This is the new covenant in my blood." Startling as it seemed, his death was to be understood as life-giving, so that each time they tapped into it, they received his nourishment: "every time you eat this bread and drink this cup, you are proclaiming his death."

Every generation, not least our own, is apt to underestimate the power of the great final act of Christ, when even as he was about to die, he somehow truly gave his very body to his friends. Without any malice, and with no deliberation, we drift into a selfish centering on our own groups and our own interests. Yet here in our midst, is the one person in history who by his death planted his life in us, and still does so. Let us be aware of the tremendous deed that happens among us, and be inspired to live in ways that are genuinely respectful, as we proclaim his death which gives us life.

Homily given on the Feast of the Body and Blood of Christ in year "A" at Stonyhurst College, Lancs.

Suicide

In two opposite ways growing young
people are isolated from the Community.

"Jews do not associate with Samaritans"
John 4:9

The sombre news that fourteen teenagers in
Bridgend have committed suicide over the last year
is bound to make us think. A deep chasm has arisen
between adult and youth; neither side seems to be
able to communicate with the other.

The isolation of young people from the adult
world arises partly from a child protection mentality
that insists that children must be kept safe from
almost every adult, so they grow up cocooned and
isolated from the grown up world, ever more and
more fettered by the very restrictions designed to
protect them. It is as though they are living in a
padded cell, locked in for their own protection.

Then when the child begins to get a degree of
independence, he or she is now seen as out of control
and a menace to the adult world. The creature who a
year ago was helpless, innocent and protected is
suddenly allocated the role of "hoody" about to kick
your head in, feral youth prowling shadowy subways
ready to attack any passer-by. In adult perception
there is at one moment, a protected species called
children, the next, menacing predators called youth.
The adult sector steers clear of either character, so
that the young person growing up stays in an isolated
world, and is forced to resort to his own devices.
Suicide spells out dramatically the isolation a person
may feel: most suicides are something to do with
loneliness.

We are told that Samaritans and Jews kept apart from each other. In the Gospel Jesus crosses that divide. He does so, not by offering the Samaritan Woman victim status – the classic modern way of dealing with someone on the other side. He does it by bluntly but lovingly offering her the truth: the truth about her and the truth about him. To this she responds, finds hope, tells everybody, and cries out "Could this be the Christ?"

Can we cross these divides that so polarise our society: between adult and youth, between inner city and suburb, between college-educated and underclass? Can we offer others truth: honest, real, straight, and offer it with love? And can we listen to what the person on the other side has to say?

Homily given on 3rd Sunday of Lent in year "A"
at Stonyhurst College, Lancs.

Do It!

Christians must enact their principles and not just affirm them.

"The second answered, 'certainly sir', but did not go."
Matthew 21:30

The slightly mixed up young man heads for India seeking enlightenment, as slightly mixed up young men tend to do. Arriving in the sacred city of Rishikesh he asks after the famous Guru, Swami Abishaktanandaji. "Where is Swami Abishaktanandaji? I heard he was in Delhi." "Yes, yes, he is in Delhi." "Oh! But someone said he has gone to the Himalayas." "Yes, yes, he is in the Himalayas!" "I was hoping to see him, is he not here?" "Yes, yes, he is here!" And at this point the famous Swami walks into the room, saffron robes, shaven head, the lot! Our amazed young man has attainted enlightenment all right; he goes beetling back to Europe to tell everyone about this fantastic Guru who is able to be in three places at the same time!

What is his mistake? It is to fail to realise that in Oriental culture politeness requires you agree with everything a person says. Claim that two and two make five, and you will be complimented on your remarkable insight; you will not be called a stupid git. We need to understand this because here in the West we do things differently: one could hardly imagine a pupil at Stonyhurst giving an assuring "Yes, yes", on being asked if he had done his studies if in fact he had not; our stiff upper lip ensures straight talking.

So the instinctive reaction of the Chief Priests and Elders is that it is the son who says "Certainly sir" who is the goody. He was polite, agreeable, impressed the bystanders with the respect he showed to his father. True, he did not do as he was asked: that is a detail, appearances were maintained. But the son who said "I will not go", contradicted his father, humiliated him before the family, showed disrespect: this is terrible!

Yet, the elders have noticed that Jesus is not fooled by fine words, this Kingdom of God he is inaugurating is the real thing, it is not a mere pretence, a piece of spin. It will only function in an authentic, in a real way. God has sent Jesus on a mission to get things done.

It is just too easy in religious matters to reduce things to mere appearances. We are all apt to do it, from the Bishop engrossed in grand ceremonies, to the numerous people who will fight to keep their lovely 400-year-old church from closure even though they never go inside it. Many a non-religious person notices the strong tendency of believers to talk big, but to do very little; they see religion as the home of hypocrisy, a sphere where all the nice things are said, but very few truly good things are done.

Let us close on something practical. Please think of one thing, perhaps quite a small thing, which you believe you should do, but in reality do not do. Fix on just one example where you are merely acting for appearance, and not doing what you say. You claim to be a Christian – do you say your prayers? You claim to care for the needy – do you act to help them? You claim to have beliefs – do you stand by them in public? You claim people should be humble enough to admit when they are wrong – do you apologise?

Homily given on 26th Sunday of Ordinary Time in year "A" at Stonyhurst College, Lancs.

A Higher King

Jesus gave a high status to the leaders of his Church.

"I tell you solemnly, whatever you bind on earth, shall be considered bound in heaven."
Matthew 18:19

James I of England was a man of education and learning. Perhaps the first person to attempt to ban smoking, with his famous quip "If God had intended men to smoke, he would have put chimneys in their heads". Unfortunately the Catholics of that time had more radical ideas: they actually tried to send James himself up in smoke with their notorious gunpowder plot of 1605, an action which did not endear them to His Britannic Majesty.

But James' great claim, which he energetically defended, was of the "Divine right of kings", a claim that kings get their authority from God, and are therefore not answerable to their subjects. It seems quite a good idea if you happen to be the king. Such a pity that in Rome the great thinker, Cardinal Robert Bellarmine was just then formulating the doctrine, that kings really get their authority from their subjects. Bellarmine attacked James' claim, and went so far as to cast doubts on the quality of the king's Latin; the which roused his majesty to reply somewhat warmly casting doubts on Bellarmine's parentage.

Nowadays we have very much taken to the idea of democracy: that rulers can make laws and enforce them, because they have been authorised to do so by the people. Indeed, those who labour under the impression that their power comes from on high, may end up in the same fate as James' son Charles who got his head chopped off.

All of this may distract us from a more fundamental truth which St Robert Bellarmine was careful to insist on. King Jesus did not get his authority from the people, in his case it really was from God. And this same power, as we heard in today's Gospel, is given by our Lord to his representatives on earth: "Whatever you bind on earth, will be considered bound in heaven".

Jesus, then, set up a unique society in his Church. One which functions with a heavenly mandate, that stretches beyond any national boundary, that is sustained by a divine power, that lays its claim on our conscience rather than our bank balance. We are uniquely privileged as Christians, to be held in unity by a high loving presence, that guides and assists us. Ours it is to be gathered together in the name of Jesus, with the assurance that he is there among us.

Therefore we do well in our own age, in which there is a rightful emphasis on the healthy nature of democracy in the secular realm, to realise that we are to be led by a higher principal in religious matters. The guidance we are given by our spiritual leaders, needs to be accepted as divinely endorsed; and by following the directions of our bishops in the practice of our faith we will surely receive heavenly blessings.

Homily given on 23rd Sunday of Ordinary Time in year "A" at Stonyhurst College, Lancs.

Holiness

God has given us His holiness, and taken our sin.

"Christ died for us while we were still sinners."
Romans 5:8

The human race has only one really deadly enemy, and that enemy is not the devil. 'Old Nick' as he has come to be called, is quite a friendly chap, easy going, enjoys life's pleasures, almost one of the family. Yes, he is a bit of a cad, and likes creating a spot of bother, but at least on the face of it he is always ready to compromise; his great aim is to get you to compromise, after all, as he so often points out, you are only human.

But there is also one who is utterly unmovable, Who when asked to state his connection with our world replies coldly "I am, who I am". In time this other one will explain that he is different from us, because he is Holy, which is to say, simply incapable of mixing with evil. As fire will not mix with water, as iron will not mix with mud, as peace will not mix with violence, so this one who is Holy cannot join in with even the least flaw, the tiniest defect, the slightest bend in our moral nature. As He states it bluntly at one point, "You must be Holy, because I the Lord your God am Holy."

Which creates a problem.

Some might like to claim that as it happens they are perfect. So no problem there.

Others might set out to make a desperate effort to be perfect, and thus OK with God. We wish them every success in their doomed endeavour.

157

But what if, in some way that we can't really explain, God swopped his holiness for our sinfulness. What if he took on our human nature, and allowed that to be the reject that his holiness must exclude, and then in that pure human nature made us holy as himself? In the words of St Paul "God made him who had no sin to be sin for us, so that in him we might become the righteousness of God."

Such an action would be almost inconceivably generous on God's part; such an action would give us an almost inconceivable benefit.

And this, St Paul is telling us, is what in his Son Jesus, God has done. We can be friends with the utterly Holy God, because he has taken our sins, and given us his holiness. Think about it.

Homily given on 11th Sunday of Ordinary Time in year "A" at Stonyhurst College, Lancs.

Rising from the Ashes

Life can rise from the ashes.

"You must worship the Lord God, and serve him alone."
Matthew 4:10

The old man was very keen on his rose bushes, and the discovery of some wood ash left over from a bonfire nearby really cheered him. "Wood ash makes very good manure," he said, as he persuaded us to collect it for him and put it at the base of his bushes.

Last Wednesday we had ash put on our foreheads to indicate two things. First, to say that is all we are, dust and ashes: no use, failed, left over, debris. But second, to indicate that God who made man and woman from dust and ashes, can create us anew, rather as that wood ash mysteriously made the rose bushes blossom.

Now it is important to grasp something here: God only remakes failed people. It is when a person sees that they have gone wrong, have ended up as useless as dust, then they may turn to God and he can rebuild them. The great hero of Israel, David, was in reality a rogue, a kind of Long John Silver of ancient times. Cunningly fomenting rebellion against King Saul, he slowly built up a power base as a guerilla leader, even allying himself with the hated Philistines. Eventually he seized power, conquered Jerusalem and set himself up there as King in the new capital. Full of pride and self confidence it seemed he could do no wrong. But in his arrogance, he fell for a woman, made her pregnant, and arranged for the murder of her husband: such was his overweening haughtiness. Only then did God show him the wrongness of his whole life, and David, bad man that he was, came to repent:

> "My offences truly I know them;" he wrote,
> "My sin is always before me.
> Against you, you alone, have I sinned;
> What is evil in your sight I have done." (Ps 51)

He came to realise that he was imbued with sin, right in his bones:

> "O see in guilt was I born,
> A sinner was I conceived." (Ps 51)

But the deeper understanding David reached was that God could make him anew, as though he were dust and ashes from the earth to be formed again:

> "O purify me, then I shall be clean;
> O wash me, I shall be whiter than snow.
> A pure heart create for me, O God,
> Put a steadfast spirit within me." (Ps 51)

Could we see into ourselves as God does, we would find but the ashes of our efforts, burnt out and useless. Such a reality is too painful to admit. But like David, if we turn to God, we find he creates us again, gives us power to do good, helps us accept ourselves, shows us the way to cope with disappointment, fills us with his Holy Spirit. And these things we can be given in Lent if we come to the sacraments: we should strive to go to the occasional weekday Mass, definitely go to Confession during this time, and make a point of saying short daily prayers.

Homily given on 1st Sunday of Lent in year "C" at Stonyhurst College, Lancs.

Her Influence

The Scriptures portray women as instigators of key events.

"Woman, my hour has not come yet."
John 2:4

Go into an Eastern Orthodox church and you will immediately be struck by the icons: religious pictures on every wall, over the ceiling, across the front. And particularly noticeable among these, the endless pictures of Mary, mother and disciple of Jesus, with her child. A stranger might well get the impression that the Christian religion is all about the worship of a woman, seeing the little child as just her protégé.

And Mary is depicted not as a mere figure of endurance, but majestically holding the future in her arms. Just as the book of Genesis depicts Eve as taking the initiative in eating the forbidden fruit, and then inducing Adam to eat also, (thus giving our man the pathetic excuse: "It was the woman you put with me; she gave me some fruit from the tree"), so these icons imply that it is Mary who is in charge and guiding events. And here at Cana it is Mary who makes the first move in leading Jesus to act. He knows, as does she, that a miracle will trigger the fateful "hour" when he must contend with Satan. She is the one who demands he take that momentous step.

In the wedding at Cana, Jesus addresses his mother simply as "woman", to mark her out as representative of womankind. He will do the same at his crucifixion when he says to Mary from the cross "Woman, this is your son, son this is your mother". Again in the book of Revelation there is a vision of a woman clothed with the sun, who bears a male child. Whilst the child is taken up into heaven, the woman remains in danger on earth pursued by the dragon, a figure of Satan.

For the Christian understanding is something like this: Jesus has won his victory, now he reigns victorious in heaven, safe from evil, safe from danger. But Mary, the woman, remains on earth, struggling with the followers of the Messiah amidst persecution, temptation, hardship, stress. Small wonder that Christians see Mary as the one who is intensely close to them, sharing their daily burdens.

And so the followers of Jesus are not wrong in seeing a woman, Mary, and she as representing womankind, as the leader who brings Jesus to embark on his saving action; and it is womankind again who live out the consequences of fidelity to Jesus. The Catholic Church, far from giving little weight to women as God's creatures, sees in Mary their key role in the divine plan. The truth is that the Church detects a mysterious strength, a sublime majesty in Mary, who accepts the cost of fidelity to Jesus, and enables his powerful love to take effect.

Those repeated icons in Orthodox churches with a woman, a slightly mournful expression on her face, holding a tiny child, who for all his majesty, is clearly dependent on her, express a profound Christian truth. In Mary and in women who share her dignity is found the source of Christian dynamism, and the strength of Christian endurance.

Homily given on 2nd Sunday of Ordinary Time in year "C" at Stonyhurst College, Lancs.

Vital Food

At times we need a special food.

"They all ate as much as they wanted"
Luke 11:17

Living in high moorland, the grouse is a bird of immense toughness. It can survive the winter in the exposed, frozen peat bogs, living on heather shoots and enduring snow storms. It is so wild and independent that no one has ever succeeded in breeding grouse in captivity. This small bird has single-handedly eliminated most of the British aristocracy, who from the glorious 12th August onwards, stand knee deep in water, under pouring rain, buffeted by icy winds trying to shoot it; with a net result of pneumonia, trench foot, rheumatism and divers associated diseases; possibly with the consolation of a few lead shot peppered brace of grouse thrown in to console their dying moments. This amazing creature has even managed to make it on to a whisky bottle, to be justly named The Famous Grouse.

But for all their legendary toughness, grouse go through a major crisis each spring. Their chicks hatch high on the moorland hills in early May, a time when at such altitudes sleet and snow are entirely possible. In the first week the tiny chicks must live off insects and grubs; they cannot eat the heather. For survival to be possible it is essential that there is a spell of warm weather, for only then do insects come out and move around. A cold spell and the entire new brood simply starve to death. Thus these birds which after a week of life can cope with anything, go through a death defying crisis in their first few days.

Our Lord knew that it is very much the same with us. Most of the time our need is for ordinary food, as was the case with that crowd in the remote country. But critically we need, and at times must have, a special food: something that will give us a strength which ordinary food cannot provide. And this is the Eucharist.

For it is the case that we need a strength morally as much as bodily. We need courage to speak the truth honestly, to resist temptation, stand by principles, endure unfairness. You cannot achieve these things on the power of bread and marmalade.

Holy Communion is that special food, it is not ordinary food. It is of divine strength, it has been called the bread of angels, it was foreshadowed by Elijah who went for forty days on a mysterious meal given to him by an angel. In the Eucharist we receive Jesus himself, the one who had such strength he could conquer death: he it is who can sustain us through any crisis.

Homily given on the feast of the Body and Blood of Christ in year "C" at Stonyhurst College, Lancs.

Unity is Harmony

True unity is more a matter of harmony
than conformity.

"That they may be one, as we are one"
John 17:21

All bodies – political parties, churches, football clubs, families – seek to be united: the advantages of unity are obvious, the tearings from divisions are palpable. "United we stand, divided we fall" as the old slogan ran. The essence of Napoleon's military tactic was to try to split the enemy line, once a crack was opened his dragoons would gallop through, and wreak havoc in the rear. The essence of Wellington's tactic at Waterloo was to keep units intact: if they could not hold a single line, they must fall back and form squares; thus united the enemy could not break them.

So it will often happen that powerful leaders will seek to impose total, uncompromising unity on society. People must think the same, they must be the same, there must be just one leader; even the smallest outbreak of diversity is to be eliminated immediately by the secret police. Thus Stalin, to take one example, ruthlessly demanded total conformity in the Soviet regime; people were not even permitted to have thoughts of their own. It has been noted that after his speeches, the vast audience would keep on clapping, because each individual was terrified of being the first to stop and thus appear out of line.

Now it is readily supposed that God has that oneness, and wishes to impose it upon his creatures. He hasn't and he doesn't. God is not one in some rigid, total, isolated way; and he does not wish us to fall into line as mini automata who mindlessly do his iron will.

There is another kind of unity, and it is the one Jesus spoke of and prayed for in his followers. It is the unity not of conformity but of harmony. Three notes may be different, but if they harmonise, they make one perfect sound. The three persons in God are one because they harmonise, not because they are the same. So when Jesus prays: "that they may be one, as we are one", he is not desiring that his disciples all say, think and do the same; no, they are to be greatly varied, but in such a way that their variety dovetails into union. Our Lord chose many diverse characters to follow him: very different personalities, each with strong desires; some are men, some are women; some are political, some are pious; some simple fishermen, some learned scholars. They must stay like that; but they need to harmonise: then they will be one.

And this, by God's grace, is what happened. In time people came to name the body of believers "the Catholic Church", that is the "all-embracing" Church, having all kinds within it. Look at the vast variety of people who make up the Church, and you will notice that its unity is a miracle of diversity.

So this is the blessing that Jesus prayed for. That we would be very different, fascinating in variety, and yet all harmonise, integrate into unity, and thus be one as God is one.

Homily given on 7th Sunday of Easter in year "C" at St. Aloysius' Glasgow.

Valiant for Truth

Edmund Campion's conviction was that truth must not be compromised for expediency.

"That they may be one, as we are one"
John 17:21

Elizabeth, daughter of Anne Boleyn and Henry VIII, had seen plenty of chaos by the time she ascended the throne in 1558. Her own mother had been executed by her father, before he went on to marry successively four more women; then the sickly child Edward VI had reigned for a few years with a Protestant government; after this Elizabeth's half sister Mary had come to the throne and made a botched attempt to restore the Catholic Religion. Now it was Elizabeth's turn: what was she to do?

Although the new queen would not have especially minded going along with the Catholic religion, she was astute enough to realise that the mood in the country by now was essentially Protestant, so she opted for a careful compromise. In the new Church of England there would be bishops, sacraments, feast days, like the Church of Rome; at the same time the Bible would replace the Blessed Sacrament in churches, and no Roman claims to appoint bishops would be accepted, it would be partly like the Calvinist regime at Geneva. The hope was that this middle of the road arrangement would be acceptable to the vast majority; as indeed proved to be the case. The Anglican way, embodied in the Church of England and its sister churches, has proved a lasting success, and its ability to accept a wide range of Christian convictions within its fold, sometimes called "The Anglican genius for compromise" can be seen as a model for tolerant, inclusive Christianity.

So it did not exactly help matters when three Jesuits: Robert Persons, Ralph Emerson and Edmund Campion landed in this country from the Continent, with the express intention of undermining the Elizabethan settlement, and persuading as many people as they could to accept the claims of the Church of Rome. Campion was well known as a leading scholar, and his cocky confident attack on the new religion published in his famous brag, got Elizabeth's government seriously worried. Would the country sink back into a horrible religious war, such as the Thirty Years War between Catholics and Protestants that would afflict Germany? Was London to become then, what Baghdad has become now: a permanent battleground for Catholics to fight Protestants, as Shiites fight Sunnis? No wonder that Campion was hunted down, and within nine months arrested, tried and executed as an enemy of the state.

So why did this highly intelligent man, and so many after him, embark on this dangerous and destructive mission? Why was he set upon dividing the religion of England, when for the first time in decades it was united, and neighbour lived in peace with neighbour? Had not Jesus prayed that his followers would be one? Campion was splitting them.

Surely it is because Jesus said that unity can only come with truth. His followers were to be united, but united in truth. And Elizabeth and her advisers were achieving a unity in which truth was compromised. In particular, Campion pointed out that the Kingdom of God cannot be ruled by the kingdom of Caesar: it respects the secular power, but is not subordinate to it. So all these claims that the monarch could be head of the Church, and that the Church of Rome was but a worldly power, must be resisted.

Campion stands as a lonely witness to honesty and integrity. Like the prophets of the Old Testament, he was hated by his fellow citizens, because he stood for the mandate given by Christ to his Apostles, when others found it politic to allow it to be appropriated by the monarch. He challenges us to be loyal to the Church that Jesus founded, to live honestly, to seek peace with everyone, but never to compromise with truth.

Homily given on 7th Sunday of Easter in year "C" at Stonyhurst College, Lancs.

Debt

Society has become trapped in debt.

"Be on your guard against avarice of any kind."
Luke 12:15

Our times are peculiar in that the pursuit of wealth has moved from being an indulgence, to being a necessity! Typically, a student today will have to incur loans to pursue degree studies, then on getting a job must strive to buy some property. To do this a mortgage is necessary, and thus the person is set on a course where, like it or not, they must desperately strive to earn as much money as possible to stay out of further debt, and repay those already incurred. Increasingly the rising generation is trapped in the need to earn frantically, because they will have to spend the best part of their lives in servicing debts.

It is generally agreed that the people of this country are on average much better off than say, fifty years ago. And yet no one seems able to enjoy wealth; they are too desperate bailing out their sinking boat to avoid drowning in debt. Many, there must be, who would very much accept our Lord's advice, who would willingly live a simple life, who can perceive that money does not buy happiness, but yet feel they have no option but to work all the hours God sends just to stay afloat.

The truth is that our society has socialised avarice: it is now embedded in the culture of living; everyone must join in or the whole system will collapse.

In this context therefore the advice of our Lord is especially hard to implement. It is not enough to take a personal decision not to be greedy; one must set one's face against the way of life that predominates: it will be necessary to be counter cultural and oppose the frantic pursuit of wealth which has become endemic.

We need to say to our age that it is under a great illusion. Money can bring temporary happiness, but only that. The material things we acquire may be useful to a degree, but they come and they go; get addicted to them and the initial thrill of having is quickly replaced by the letdown of their shallowness. Our pursuit of wealth is not only producing hot air in the global warming sense, it is frankly a load of hot air as a vehicle for delivering happiness.

As we know, Jesus invited some followers to abandon everything and follow him. This is not the call given to everyone; but each of us should have the mentality. That is, we should be able to recognise that Jesus' invitation was a liberation: that he was showing his friends how to live without the burden of earthly cares. And thus there is a duty on us to oppose the modern adulation of wealth; its constant emphasis on more; its claim to solve any problem via money, its dreadful creation of the debt-ridden society.

Homily given on 18th Sunday of Ordinary Time in year "C" at Stonyhurst College, Lancs.

Drugs

A serious drug problem may suck other family members into its web.

"He would have filled his belly with the husks the pigs were eating"
Luke 15:17

It must be a terrible blow to parents when they realise their son or daughter is addicted to drugs. First the slight signs of bad temper and moodiness, then losing the job or abandoning college, the admission eventually by him or her to being hooked, the pathetic pleas for cash to pay off drug debts, with hysterical claims of reform in the future. The parents seeing their child's health deteriorate, sinking into insanity, hospital, clinic, depression: a no hope scenario.

But waiting in the wings is an even nastier possibility. What if this dreadful road to addiction becomes a model for the other children? Parents can watch on Television News a character like Pete Docherty being taken to court, and be horrified to see that he attracts a bevy of excited teenagers enthusiastically milling around their hero; insanely perceiving him as a role model. To a parent the deepest fear is that the addict child will contaminate the family with his lifestyle, and the fate of one will spread to become the fate of the others.

Thus it is not surprising that some parents, determined to save what they can of their wrecked family's life, make the drastic choice to cut off the addict from the home. As with foot and mouth disease, it is a matter of being ruthless, in order to protect the ones not yet contaminated. Their addict

172

daughter must be left to destroy herself alone; in no way must she get access to the home again.

The oddness of the story Jesus tells, is that the father does not take that route. His elder son points out that he is acting crazy in letting that wretch loose on the home and the farm, after all the havoc he has already caused, but the father persists and takes him back. You could perhaps say that he is a doting parent, too sentimental to take a stand against this feckless son; but surely Our Lord wants us to see here a healing power at work, that makes the father's act not soppy, but wise.

When Jesus is criticised for mixing with the equivalent of gun-carrying gangs, with prostitutes, with drug addicts, he does not justify it with some liberal talk about inclusion, diversity or tolerance. No, these people are dangerous, they may well contaminate others. And this is precisely why our Lord portrays himself as a doctor: a person who can mix with disease without succumbing to it. Jesus is claiming a healing power that enables him to hang out with bad people, yet help them and heal them.

The challenge to us is two-fold. Do you believe that if you were ever in a total mess, be it through drugs or whatever, he still has a place for you in God's Kingdom, where still you can be healed? Second are you able to believe that in a real crisis you will be given power to help a desperate failed friend; power of a heavenly order well beyond your natural abilities?

Homily given on 24th Sunday of Ordinary Time in year "C" at Stonyhurst College, Lancs.

Care for Creation

God has entrusted us to care for the world
he created: we have a duty to treat it with
respect.

***"Till the flood came and swept
them all away"***
Matthew 24:39

People who live in dry or desert conditions are often
much more afraid of water than we are. In our wet
climate, rain, water, rivers are always close, but in the
desert when it rains a drastic change takes place. Dry
river beds, called wadis, which seem to be just part
of the sandy rocky countryside suddenly become
raging torrents, and animals, people, tents in their
path are swept away. Thus the very people who spend
large amounts of time searching for water, are the
most terrified by it when it really rains. For people
of these regions stories like that of Noah would be
part of the folklore passed down from generation to
generation, with its underlying message, do not mess
with nature. The folk tale is taken over in the Bible
to become "Don't mess with nature, and do not mess
with God the author of nature."

As our Lord said, people get used to things being
as they are, and then get shocked if drastic change
comes: they do not anticipate what is inevitable,
because they are not used to it. And could not this
be the case with climate change? For a long time we
have acted as though we can do just what we like
with God's creation, as regards its forests, its minerals,
its fossil deposits; yes and as regards our very own
bodies, that critical apex of the created order. Nature
is made by God good, and thus has a dynamism, a

character, a self-regulating tendency to assert itself: treat it with contempt and it will fight back. What is more its reaction is liable to be sudden, unexpected and drastic: like a torrential flood in a desert wadi.

And maybe we, as people of faith, should be especially concerned with this underlying abuse of nature that may be leading to global warming: it is the modern industrial attitude that we can do just as we wish with the world, and are answerable to no one. We are creatures who have been placed on this earth to care for creation; on us is the responsibility to look after it. What is more if we do not care for creation about us, the chances are that we will not care for that creature who is its centre: the human person. And it is we who will disappear in the flood.

Homily given on 1st Sunday of Advent in year "A"
at Stonyhurst College, Lancs.

"He Who Is"

God is real, and must not be confused with imaginary things.

"Say 'I AM has sent me to you'"
Exodus 3:14

The gods of our imagination are not to be messed with, as a vicar who went into a primary school to announce that there was no Father Christmas quickly discovered. Having explained helpfully to the children that even Lapland was not big enough to store millions of toys, that shipping them by reindeer all on the same night would require a sleigh weighing hundreds of tons, that the speed Father Christmas would need to travel to get the job done in eight hours would heat everything so much the toys would incinerate, and the sleigh implode: he waited for their reaction. The children burst into tears.

Moses believed in the gods alright, as any simple person does. Even as a child you thought that those presents which appeared at Christmas must have been given by someone. Doubtless a nice old buffer if he gives presents for free, and he must be used to the cold if he comes round in the middle of winter. Thus with the help of your parents you managed to work out that there must be some heavenly old chap out there called Father Christmas.

Therefore Moses got a shock that day when he encountered not one of those nice gods that we invent for our day to day needs: this God was not one of our gods. This God is; he exists; Moses had not invented Him; nor had anyone else. This God will impact upon Moses, on Egypt, and on the

Hebrews. So Moses is told quite bluntly that this God is to be known as "He Who Is".

Moses was shown that the strange God was not a part of nature. For whereas with us a fire only burns by consuming its fuel, the sign of "He Who Is" comes in the form of a fire that needs no material resource. He exists of himself, not in dependence on nature.

It is of great importance that there is a being quite independent of us, with whom we must connect without making him part of ourselves. Because our relations with people are all too apt to take the form of manipulating others, make them extensions of ourselves, or at least get them to fit in with our plans. This is to say, we are apt to treat others not as persons: independent, autonomous, to be respected in their own right, but as things: items, possibly useful, possibly obstructing our path. So often we fail to accept the otherness of persons. Now that Moses has come across one who is completely other, he can start to learn the painful lesson that his fellow men and women must be respected in their independence too.

This time of Lent is one for us to discover "He Who Is". It is time for us to cease living off figments of our imagination.

Homily given on 3rd Sunday of Lent in year "C" at Stonyhurst College, Lancs.

Teaching

In the Church Jesus Christ founded
we will find the truth.

*"Baptise them in the name of …,
and teach them to observe all the
commands I gave you."*
Matthew 28:29

Having lost the battle of Worcester in 1651, the son
of King Charles I was in a desperate state. Two years
earlier the Roundheads had executed his father, and
now Oliver Cromwell had so utterly defeated the
young prince that as he fled from Worcester the only
prospect seemed to be of capture and death.

By a most extraordinary providence the young
Charles came into the hands of the one group of
people who could help him: the Catholics. Persecuted
for the last hundred years, their priests sentenced to
death even for saying Mass, this small and dwindling
community only survived through an extensive
system of underground contacts and closely knit
loyalty to each other, together with the ingenious
hiding holes they constructed to conceal priests.
Boscobel House near Brewood sheltered the Prince
for a time, then he was passed on to Moseley Old
Hall near Wolverhampton. Here he not only used
the hiding hole but actually met a Catholic Priest,
Fr John Huddleston, and saw the secret chapel.

Although the mother of the Prince, Henrietta
Maria, was a devout Catholic, Charles had very little
knowledge of our beliefs, for the Puritan authorities
had taken extreme measures to save him from any
Popish influence, even to the point of insisting that
his very cradle had to be rocked by approved

Protestants. But in any case the Prince may well have been quite confused about religious belief, because the England of the civil war was one not only of political but also of religious chaos. Levellers thought every person should be the same – no priests, no bishops, no kings; Covenanters believed in elders but not bishops, the Church of England was marginalised by the extreme Puritan factions, whilst the extraordinary Fifth Monarchy men did not want a government of any kind, maintaining that Jesus Christ was about to come and rule the country.

Trapped in Moseley Old Hall with the Roundheads urgently searching for him, the prince had time on his hands. Fr Huddleston was able to show him the Catholic catechism: Charles was impressed: "I have not seen anything more plain and clear," he remarked, "the arguments here drawn are so conclusive, I do not see how they can be denied." In an age when private judgement was the great slogan, the fugitive prince suddenly found a group of people who accepted a teaching Church, and he recognised the power and authority of its carefully assembled arguments. His reaction was like that of the crowds to Jesus: "Here is a teaching that is new," they said, "and with authority behind it."

We are today, on Trinity Sunday, seeing the launch of the new Catholic Catechism. It shows the Church still following the command of the Lord to teach us to observe all the commands he gave us; and reminds us that we do not get or keep our faith merely by our own thoughts and ideas: we are dependent on that vessel which with centuries of experience and care, and aided by the divine light of the Holy Spirit, seeks to instruct us in the way of Christ. So fundamental is this work, that the Church is often called a mother, nurturing Christ in us by her teaching and by her sacraments.

Thanks to the help of his friends Charles eventually escaped to the continent and in 1660 was invited back to England to become King Charles II. But the true end of the tale was in 1685: as he lay dying, the King indicated that he wanted to embrace the Catholic Faith: the same Fr John Huddleston whom he had met at Moseley Old Hall was smuggled into the palace and having received him gave him the Last Rites. Charles died in peace and calm: could it be that the catechism he had examined years before had sown the seed which now came to fruition in his last moments on earth?

Homily given on Trinity Sunday of year "B"
at Saints Peter and Paul, Mitcham.

A Lazy Creation

We will have a better understanding of creation if we see God as an artist rather than a mechanic.

"Observe the Sabbath day and keep it holy"
Exodus 20:8

The most interesting thing about the creation of the world in October 4004 BC was that it took place at 10 o'clock in the morning! Bishop James Ussher, who thought he knew a thing or two about these matters, has let us have his own exact calculation of the event.

If you or I were creating a Galaxy or two, we would hardly wait until 10am before clocking on. In our steam driven age everything must be done frantically; planning groups set up, targets decided upon, zero tolerance of any failure.

Indeed our age can hardly give its approval to the lackadaisical approach of the Creator, who having begun late, worked for a mere six days, and then took a day off! Not just took a day off; he did nothing whatever, just lazed around for twenty-four hours. Hardly an efficient way to create a universe! A point brought out by any environmental audit or inspection of the job: our world is quite clearly half-baked, half-finished, half-planned.

There is a difference, is there not, between the way God does things, and the way the modern age does things. God creates for enjoyment; our age neurotically works for efficiency and productivity. God's motto could be stated in that deceptively profound saying of the master of paradox "If a job is worth doing, it is worth doing badly." Such a notion is heresy to twentieth-century progress.

And hence it is that Sunday has moved from a day of rest to a day of slavery; everyone is racing around to get more done: work, shopping, and all the other things. No one can relax; we have chosen neurotic activity to make ourselves feel needed; we are unable to enjoy anything, least of all our own creative actions. How far are we from that profound saying of Eastern Religion "all this world must be pervaded by a Lord, renounce it, and enjoy it."?

It is a fact, here as elsewhere, that the numbers coming to Mass on Sunday are dropping. Of course there are many reasons for this, and a lot of people have little control over their time on Sunday or any other day. But we should try to persuade our friends that they should come precisely because it is not a target, an achievement, some job done. We should tell them that coming to Mass on Sunday is a complete waste of time; and that he who made the starry skies thought his work good enough to waste time over: a very creative act; let us imitate it.

Homily given on 3rd Sunday of Lent in year "B" at St. Aloysius' Glasgow.

Christmas in Privet Drive

People who are rather different are not really welcome.

"Because there was no room at the inn"
Luke 2:7

The man and young girl looked weary and bedraggled as they finally reached Privet Drive and sought out the house of their relatives. No doubt the Dursleys would not exactly welcome them, but in the circumstances, perhaps they would let them stay for a night or two.

Unfortunately the immediate reaction of Arthur Dursley, when they rang the bell, was edgy and defensive. "Wot dau yau want?" was his gruff Black Country greeting. Dursley had heard some of the stories about this couple, and he did not like them at all. A down to earth, practical man, into the manufacture and distribution of drills, he did not care for all this miracle stuff: an angel with a message, a miraculous baby, a promised king. It struck him as silly, even dangerous: Dursley liked to stay with what was familiar.

He did let them in; but as they sat down in the living room, a black cloud was overshadowing Dursley's face; he was not comfortable at all. Fantasies were haunting his mind that he could not quite formulate, they were unsettling him and making him uneasy. Dursley was worried, very worried.

Although he could not pin-point what bothered him, Dursley was in fact frightened that this rumoured child would unsettle things. To his way of thinking the world was made of good and bad, carefully balanced against each other; you were

183

alright so long as you left things alone. Even though he claimed not to believe in it, the idea of someone coming down from heaven was unnerving: it could easily overturn the way things were. And he knew that there were dark forces that would not take kindly to an invasion of their earthly empire. Not that Dursley himself was a bad man: he was hard working, honest, looked after his family, cleaned the car every Sunday: he was a straight, down to earth sort. It was precisely his practical nature that gave him an instinctive feeling that this whole business was dangerous: did that young girl sitting opposite him have any idea of what she was getting into?

The tension in the room was increasing, not helped by Petunia, Dursley's wife, getting agitated at the thought that their son Dudley might have to share the small house with a new-born baby. Dudley was a delicate child, she was convinced he had to be very carefully protected. But then in her agitation, an idea struck her:

"Yau car stay 'ere, there aye room in our 'ouse!" Then pointing accusingly at the girl's bulging tummy she blurted out "yau go and ave that babby up the garden, in the shed there, so no one ull see yau." Arthur concurred, and pathetically offered them a carton of milk to take.

Silently Joseph and the girl walked down the garden to the shed. In a sense the girl preferred it this way. She had come to understand that what she was going through was not usual: she had heard an angel, she was to bear an eternal king, she had been overshadowed by the Spirit from on High. All of these things would hardly fit in with the small world of the Dursleys; perhaps they were better by themselves.

And so the baby was born; they made the most

of it. As Joseph rummaged around seeking some warming things he looked out and saw that it had snowed: everything was covered in white. Somehow that snow seemed like another message from that other world: it, too, had come from above; was white and pure, like everything up there; so silent and peaceful, able to speak without saying words; and all things were covered by it, making a marvellous fresh start.

Yes, there was no doubt, a new world had begun: they could be at peace in this one, even if they did not belong in the other.

Homily given at Midnight Mass on Christmas Day
at St. Aloysius' Glasgow.

A Wedding

Marriage has many challenges, and
needs God's help.

*"Be kind enough to have pity on her
and on me."*
Tobit 8:7

The reading we had from the book of Tobit gives us
a charming prayer of Sarah and Tobias on their
wedding night, as they ask for God's blessing, and
protection on their future. As I will explain in a
minute they have very strong motives indeed for
seeking the protection of God, but in any case one
could well imagine the dangers that such a couple
would have faced in those times.

If you have read the book of Tobit you will
know that Sarah and Tobias are actually nervous for
a very specific reason: Tobias is in fact the eighth
husband of Sarah, the previous ones having died!
Slightly unfortunate you may think, but what would
concentrate your mind if you were in Tobias' shoes is
that the previous seven all died on the wedding
night! No wonder he is praying for protection. Of
course the book is a kind of religious romance, and
we are told that these mysterious deaths were really
all the work of a wicked demon, to make Sarah seem
a murderess. Only God can protect them from this
demon: hence their prayer for his protection.

Nevertheless, given that they lived in an age of
war and disease, simply to survive would be
wonderful; and we notice that the main point of
their prayer is that God will protect and preserve
them throughout life: "Be kind enough" Tobias prays,

"to have pity on her and on me, and bring us to old age together."

Today we hardly see marriage as threatened by plague, war, or revolution (although sadly it is so threatened in some countries). Nowadays, marriage is more likely to break up for internal reasons, where husband and wife simply cannot get on together, and eventually in despair separate and go their different ways. And there can be little doubt that modern marriage is very much in danger of such breakdown, as the weary divorce statistics make all too evident. Could we call on God to protect us from these modern hazards, as Tobias and Sarah pleaded to be spared from the dangers of their time?

So, Andrea and Dunstan, even though you do not commence your marriage under great physical dangers, you will need both God's protection and blessings to persevere, when modern marriage comes under such great pressures, and many couples struggle to keep their relationship together. The challenge you face is "Can you make your marriage succeed?" And part of the answer to this must be "Only with the help of God". Today then, at this Nuptial Mass, you seek God's favour on your future; with his help you can have a happy marriage, you can spread joy around you, you can reach old age together, you can come into God's Kingdom at the end of your lives. We pray for all these things.

Homily given at a Wedding in St. Aloysius' Glasgow.

The Seed of Faith

As the saying goes: 'The blood of
the martyrs is the seed of faith.'

*"One of those from whom people
hide their faces"*
Isaiah 53:3

The rain was coming down heavily as the three
prisoners were tied to two hurdles outside the Tower
of London: Ralph Sherwin and Alexander Briant to
one, Edmund Campion on the other. One end of
each hurdle was hitched to the back of a horse, whilst
the other simply trailed along the muddy cobbled
street, bumping up and down as it was dragged.
Campion, tortured and emaciated, now wet, mud-
spattered and mis-shapen must have seemed like a
drowned rat; something the onlookers gazed at, some
pityingly, others curiously; these events always drew
large crowds.

Arriving at Tyburn Gallows, located very close
to today's Marble Arch in central London, Campion
laboriously climbed the steps, along with the other
two. Shaking and weak he tried to make himself
heard to the muttering mass of onlookers. "We have"
he said, "been made a spectacle for God, to angels,
and to men." The people looked up at the pathetic
figure, many not knowing who he was or what he
did.

For most would hardly know that this man had
once had outstanding prospects: tipped at Oxford to
become a leading figure in the new Church, with
even the Earl of Leicester as his patron. He had
mysteriously left all that, gone to the continent, been
reconciled with the Catholic Faith, joined the

Society of Jesus, and finally at great peril to his life, had landed in England to preach religion as a Catholic priest. Even after his arrest, he had been considered important enough to be brought before Queen Elizabeth and offered a glittering future if only he would leave all this Papist stuff behind. His refusal sealed his fate.

Now on the scaffold he stood a dismal figure, as the people stared up at him before the execution. For many this was but a show; they watched with curiosity to see how brave he would be in the last moments; for others it was a sad sight: three people being mangled to death. For a few it was more serious: some ministers desperately tried to get him to admit he was in the wrong, and that he was indeed part of a grand plot to get England invaded by the Pope. They got nowhere with their harangues, Campion and his companions were beyond all that stuff. But one man in the crowd, Henry Walpole, was genuinely concerned. A bit of a wit, something of a playboy, clever, easy-going, one of the lads, he nevertheless had his serious side, and was filled with awe at the courage and integrity of Campion and the others. As they carried out the executions on the three, cutting them down while still alive, and then butchering the bodies, a spot of blood from Campion spattered onto Walpole's coat.

Shortly after, Henry Walpole left England, crossed the sea, became a priest and returned as Campion once had done. Thirteen years on, after terrible sufferings, he was executed at York, suffering the same fate on the gallows as Campion had undergone.

It illustrated very vividly the prophetic words Campion had addressed to the Queen and Privy Council when he had landed in England:

"Be it known to you that we have made a league… cheerfully to carry the cross you shall lay upon us, and never despair your recovery, while we have a man left to enjoy your Tyburn, or to be racked with your torments, or consumed with your prisons. The expense is reckoned, the enterprise is begun; it is of God, it cannot be withstood. So the faith was planted: so it must be restored."

Homily given at Stonyhurst College, feast of St. Edmund Campion, 1 December 2008.